REHEARSING YOUR MISTAKES

ÁNGEL SIMAL

Aotearoa, May 2014

Table of Contents

FOREWORD

Mistakes are inherent in any practice. Magic is no exception to this rule. However painful it may be for the person who makes it, it must be recognised as having an educational value and, for those who know how to take advantage of it, a creative opportunity. This is the problem of the handling to which the magician must submit when an unforeseen event occurs, whatever its cause. To miss a manipulation should not be attributable to a random mistake, but frankly, to a mistake that lies with the magician. One can and should blame oneself for this. The vital thing in this matter is to have foreseen this eventuality beforehand and to have found a way to avoid it. It is purely a matter of work and fine-tuning his act.

The handling of an external event that disturbs the act can add value to it, provided that it is mastered or, better still, appropriated. I will never forget this one spectator with a generous laugh during my whistle act in La Coruña in 2010. The rapport I was able to establish with this person, whom no one could see, but whom everyone could hear, became a moment of intense sharing and the driving force behind greater success.

Angel Simal offers us today a tool for reflection and management that every magician should have. He analyses the workings of a seemingly undesirable event, which we must live with and ideally know how to take advantage of. Through a meticulous and exhaustive work, he proves to us to what extent the unfathomable can become an opportunity. As my friend Professor Dessi likes to say: "The fault is condemnable, the error is forgivable, the incident exploitable."

Norbert Ferré

PREFACE

Dear friend, you are now holding in your hands one of those books that fall inside the category of "magic theory". This is a study I developed on a topic that I felt it was worth taking a dive into: the magician's mistakes.

When people ask if you have ever messed up on stage, what do you answer? This is never an easy question, especially if it makes you recall uncomfortable situations from your past.

Perhaps you never made a mistake on stage yet. Good on you! However, I encourage you to keep on reading as once you are in trouble, it will be late to take precautions.

The audience appreciates attending a professional show in which the artist never loses control, even when the elements are against him. In these pages, you will have the opportunity to reflect on how to overcome your fears and how to act properly in unexpected situations.

I do not intend to reinvent the wheel with *Rehearsing Your Mistakes*, but to help you tidy some ideas and concepts. I would like to make you think without establishing any dogmas. We often do not realise that we could easily avoid some situations if we did a proper risk assessment during our rehearsals.

Then, I will explain some concepts around some magician's acts that include artificial mistakes. I will show you how you could use a temporary failure as a tool to get more significant reactions from your spectators, and you will understand why they enjoy it so much.

If you buy a theory book like this one, it is perhaps because you are already interested in taking some time to reflect on how you can become a better performer or public speaker. I can assure you that all the time you invest in learning theory and reflection will gradually boost your skills and your career.

I also hope that you will enjoy the chapter where I talk about creativity. Not only the greatest minds invent new stuff, and perhaps you have already created a little something yourself. As Henry Van

Dyke would say, the woods would be very silent if no birds sang there except those singing best.

I advise you to read slowly, try to stop on each idea to reflect for a little while and read only one chapter per day. This study does not end with the last page of this book, but it extends to the notes you will write down on your notebook. If you do not have one ready, go to the store, and get yourself one as soon as possible.

See you on the next page.

Ángel

0. The Bicycle

"One should never have fear to lose, in fact, in my honours I can count more defeats than wins." – Miguel Induráin

I was really enjoying the feeling of speed. The wind was caressing my face, and I was even opening my mouth a little to swallow some air so I could feel it inside while I was still pedalling with energy... but suddenly... thud! A new fall!

I had just turned seven, and my parents had just given me the greatest gift: a brand new blue BH and a whole summer ahead of me to learn to ride a bicycle.

It was already my third day enjoying the great present, and my knees were already showing some small wounds, while my hands were not offering a much different look.

Every day, the afternoon snack took the flavour of the ground of my grandparents' backyard, and my frustration increased inevitably with every fall.

Oh! How the wounds stung!

Every night I dreamt with outings to the local hill with my friends. I could not wait for those dreams to become real adventures.

I often watched other kids riding their bikes, and it did not look that hard. However, my first attempts with the blue BH did not go well. Fail after fail, fall after fall.

My uncles were frequently giving me encouraging words and pieces of advice. Soon, I took for granted that there was no other way of learning how to ride a bicycle but trying it again and again.

I knew the theory quite well: first, I would give it a gentle push with my foot on the ground, then I had to hold tight the bike's handlebar and finally, never stop pedalling!

However, once on the bike I had to control the speed with the pedalling pace, I had to turn the handlebar softly on the bends, I had to lift my hip slightly every time I wanted to go over an obstacle, I had to pull the brakes firmly for the rear wheel but very softly for the front one... literally a million things to consider!!

And that was not all I had to manage. There were factors other than me and the bicycle which also had to be taken into account: on rainy days it was more challenging to control the bike, the puddles were treacherous, the stones changed places when I was not looking, my grandfather's dog could never stand still... an endless list of random factors!

My seven-year-old version was amazed by the cyclists on television. They never stopped pedalling while they drank water with one hand, and in the meantime, with the other one they controlled the handlebars... and all that at more than 40 kilometres per hour!

With blood, sweat and tears, little by little, I eventually started to learn from my own mistakes.

Still, I was upset when I fell off the bike due to a mistake that I had already made before. New mistakes were still disappointing, but I started to take mental note of everything that had happened, and I always clenched my teeth to climb back with renewed enthusiasm on the saddle.

I spent my days practising and memorizing every stone on the track. Also, I made sure my family kept the dog under control while I was on the bike.

There came a day when my mother wanted to see my progress. I got super nervous, and during the "talent show" I could barely manage to pedal a few meters without falling. That felt terrible. Another new lesson to learn: focus well on what you are doing no matter who is watching.

Day and night, I was obsessed with the idea of getting to ride a bicycle like the other children I had seen on the street. It was never my wish to run the Vuelta de España. That was clear to me. I just wanted to enjoy pedalling without my physical integrity being affected and without making a fool of myself.

The following week, the demonstration before my mother went much better. I kept nervous, but as I had expected it, I was able to concentrate better. I did not try anything complicated that day, and I managed to complete a couple of laps on the track without any accident. That was my first small triumph.

The days went by, and I kept practising every afternoon, I started to "simply know" what worked on the bike and what were not that good ideas that ended up with me on the ground.

By the end of that summer, my bike skills had grown considerably, and I was already pedalling with great confidence. It even allowed me to speak to my observers while riding the bike. I was so proud of myself!

One day, I noticed that my mother was secretly watching me during my practice, and I decided to try a little mischief: I started by taking one of the track's straight lines. Then, I gradually increased the speed, and as a consequence, the handlebar began a disturbing rattle as

13

the bicycle ran over the stones so fast. Right when my Mum was starting to yell at me to pedal more slowly, I turned the steer abruptly to the side while pulling hard from the rear wheel brake. The bike, how could it be otherwise, skidded on the track, making a noise that seemed heavenly music in my ears.

It all ended with me standing in the centre of the track, with one foot on the ground and the other one still on a bicycle pedal. My hands held the handlebar firmly, and I looked up at my mother with the broadest grin.

She had thought that I had lost control of the bike and that I was going to get a new smack... But instead, I made an unexpected manoeuvre that showed my control over the vehicle.

I was feeling great! Although smiling, my mother did not know whether to scold me for recklessness or congratulate me on my skills. My uncles could not help laughing at my little bravado.

That was a summer that I will never forget. With trial and error, and a lot of practice, I learned to ride a bicycle. The hits every time I made a mistake were not only physical but also mental. I was indeed truly fortunate to have people around me to cheer me up and give me some piece of advice. With them by my side, I always felt that everything was more manageable.

Of course, the falls from that summer were not the only ones I have ever suffered from a saddle. Over the years, new bicycles arrived, and I enjoyed new day trips. Some of those trips included the occasional small accident, like the day a truck pushed me off the road, the day my saddle broke halfway on the river track, the day I crossed paths with a terrified rabbit in the middle of the bush, etc. All those were falls to which little or nothing I could have done, mainly events based on circumstantial bad luck, anecdotes of the cyclist.

Common sense, observation and conversations with friends have also taught me how to keep a bike in good condition. In the end, the correct operation of this prop depends on my care. A well-oiled chain, well-calibrated brakes, tires in perfect condition, etc., they make up a list of external factors that I can control to a certain extent.

Luckily, nowadays, my confidence when pedalling is excellent. But experience has taught me always to be alert, anticipate and assess the risks that may arise during the route before leaving, and use my knowledge and skills to improvise as best as I can in unexpected situations to avoid an accident.

For me, enjoying a ride means a lot of things. It means feeling the wind on my face, admiring the landscape, chatting and laughing with my friends, going down the slopes at full speed... and all this I could never do if I did not ride with trust.

...

Back then, my seven-year-old version could not imagine that a few years later, I would strive to learn how to be a good artist on stage. A new passion ran through my veins like a virus that flooded my entire body. I wanted to enjoy performing on a stage and to play with the spectators while transporting them to a fantastic world.

I started to prepare the hydrogen peroxide and the plasters just in case.

Fortunately, learning to be a good artist did not involve blood, but it did take a lot of sweat and tears. The road was long, and the wounds turned out to be mental.

My new goal was to become a good magician, but I already had an ace up my sleeve: I knew that I would have to learn many things and not only to do the tricks right...

1. The Mistake

"In the Arab world, every work of art has a tiny flaw, so that it does not sacrilegiously compete with the perfection of God." – World Without End (Ken Follet)

Since we are little, human beings quickly learn that things do not have to go the way we always want. We can fall and hurt ourselves, but we can do it with a new lesson learned when we get back on our feet. A life that always followed the expected script, without any unwelcome turns, would ultimately be boring. Don't you think?

Magicians call it a mistake when they refer to the outcome of an effect that falls outside of the script, and it has not met the audience's expectations.

In my definition, I exclude the expectations of the magician because I think that even if things do not develop as expected, as long as the crowd is satisfied, nobody will ever talk about any magician's mistake.

In the same way that when you learn how to ride a bike, you must experience falls and bruise your knees; in magic, you will also find unexpected obstacles that will attack your morale. We must not let ourselves be cursed by them because we will be better artists once they are overcome.

Mistakes make us get off the tracks where we were travelling comfortably, and suddenly, they put us in front of a road that we did not even know it existed. This new route can lead us into an unknown world of new possibilities. Then, we have the choice of getting depressed or seeing it as an opportunity to reinvent ourselves. If you are interested in innovation, then you are interested in failing.

Scientists are used to dealing with failure daily. We should mirror them. No one can invent things that work well from the very beginning every day. There are even some discoveries that happen "by mistake".

Percy Spencer was an American engineer who changed the lives of many people around the world. He was a magnetron specialist. One day, when this engineer was investigating a radar failure, he noticed that a chocolate bar in his pocket got utterly melted. That led him to make a connection in his head. After implementing some adjustments to the magnetron, he successfully made popcorn.

Do you think Percy Spencer was devastated by such an unexpected turn of the script (research)? Of course not, and years later he was granted the patent for the invention of the microwave.

Most people are obsessed with getting things right, and in a way, it makes sense based on the education we receive. From a young age, we are censored by doing things "wrong". However, I am suggesting that you do not turn your back on failure. Try to learn from it, and I guarantee you will improve in the future.

Total failure only comes when you give up your dreams; that is why it is vital to get up after every fall.

Can it happen to anyone?

There is no immunity from mistakes and failure. All magicians, from beginners to world-class illusionists, are exposed to them.

The higher you climb, the harder you fall. I am sure you heard that before. Falling badly once could make anyone's career bite the dust. Let us be humble and careful because we never know when or where things will not go our way.

An artist's career is a cross-country one, and we should never be discouraged by unforeseen events, but we should learn from them for the future.

Why do they happen?

The question we always certainly ask ourselves when something did not go as we expected: "Why? Why? Why?"

The answer is simple and very straightforward. We cannot always control everything 100 per cent.

When our chemistry teacher told us to solve a problem in my student days, she always added in her statement the conditions of the environment for the experiment. It was not the same to work under normal conditions (0 degrees Celsius and 1 atmosphere) as under different ones. The magician will also find that the rehearsals' conditions are surely different from the conditions in a performance with a real audience.

Some reader may be thinking that it can be impossible to know exactly under which conditions we are going to perform. Right, but we can prepare as best as we can. This way, we will shield ourselves before the unknown to get away with adversity.

Consequences of a mistake: magician-audience-show

A mistake on stage immediately affects us. It makes us lose focus, and it cuts off the transmission of emotions to the audience. Many times, spectators realise that something has gone wrong because of the magician's nonverbal language, and from that moment on, it will be impossible for us to deny the situation.

Look at the image that serves as the cover of this book. You will find a magician reaching inside his hat with one hand. He has not produced anything yet, but his body language reveals that something must not have gone as he expected.

As Marco Tempest says in one of his talks, the audience does not come to the theatre to watch the magician die, shred by some spears or shattered by a saw, but to see him triumph and dance with the girl. I agree with Marco that the best stories are the ones that end well. If the magician fails and conveys his grief to the crowd, the crowd will suffer with him, and nobody will go home happy.

The impact of a mistake on the show may be greater or lesser depending on the magician's reaction. Some flaws will be of great importance depending on when they happen or on the reason for their existence. However, an inadequate response to a small mistake could trigger a chain reaction that could end the entire show.

The final verdict will always come from the audience. That is how we will know how right or wrong we have done it. For the customer who hires us, the audience's satisfaction will always be the most important thing. Do not forget it.

How do we feel after a mistake?

In our nature, humans feel nervousness, frustration, and anger because of the mistakes we make. We will reveal our shame on stage as we start moving more quickly and out of control, trying to explain what happened and making excuses that will possibly be ridiculous.

As for ridicule, it is something we choose to feel ourselves. As we will see later, this will be the feeling that will invade us if we come across a situation that we were already aware that could happen, and we did nothing to remedy it. Capital sin!

A good risk assessment could help us to respond with more serenity and self-control. Certain situations may be so remote that, if given, there is no choice but to accept them and to move forward.

How should we react when messing up on stage?

For the audience, our reaction to our mistakes will be far more critical than the errors themselves.

It is not easy to behave with the right attitude when a mistake happens. It requires a level of self-control that we can only be achieve with some training. We can only gain the right naturalness to carry out our actions with a lot of experience and good knowledge of oneself and the show itself.

The goal should be not to let the mistakes lead us towards total failure in our show.

In a limit situation, a good magician will use a proper obliteration parenthesis (Ascanio's parenthesis of forgetfulness in Spanish) to downplay the mistake. However, some magicians could use the mess to take advantage of it during the rest of the performance.

How can we prevent or minimise the risk of messing up?

Perhaps, a more straightforward way than learning how to overcome a mistake could be learning how to minimize the likelihood of something happening off the script.

That is why we should reflect on why these situations happen.

What is the source of our mistakes?

The number of sources and reasons can be endless. We could classify them in many ways, but for me, the logical thing would be to do it in avoidable or unavoidable reasons. Then, we could split both as related to the magician or the environment.

With unforeseen situations that could not have been avoided, we should not worry anymore. We should only analyse them later to find possible ways out for the future.

Of course, we will commit a mortal sin, if we do not work so that the avoidable situations never happen to us again, and more rightly if the root cause of the mistake is related to the artist himself.

Among the random factors that can escape part of our control are those related to the theatre, its technicians and the proper handling of lights, music, etc. There is little we can do about those. At the very least, let's try to make it easier for the staff. Let's explain very well and with patience what we expect from them, and let's be friendly and kind. All of this will have a positive impact on our own benefit.

The more random factors are surrounding a show, the greater the risk of something unexpected influencing the magician's presentation.

An outdoor stage will have many more potential risks than a room or a theatre. As long as we are aware of it, the fewer surprises we will take.

Once, I met a magician who always carried his material in duplicate: scissors, decks of cards, batteries, silks and much more. We could fall into the hypochondria if we pretended to do that with all our props. In the end, we could need bringing a spare magician just in case...

The environment can become fanciful and always give us a surprise with something unexpected. However, as we are good artists, our presentation must be immaculate. We can only achieve this with a lot of practice and rehearsal.

Practice and Rehearsal

Eugene Burger, the great magician from Illinois, has often explained the difference between practice and rehearsal:

"The practice aims to achieve mastery of a technique based on repetition. First, at the intellectual level and then, at a physical level, we will absorb the necessary manipulative techniques and our routines' moves. Once at this point, we will be ready to rehearse."

The rehearsal involves a preliminary phase of analysis of the conditions of the performance environment. We should try to forecast what will happen around us, and we should rehearse the routine as if we were in those expected conditions. We should tell the story in the same way as before our audience, we should make the same pauses, we should tell the same jokes, and we should greet in the same way at the end. With the rehearsal, we will achieve the mastery of acting.

However, no matter how much analysis and how much rehearsal we do, **we will never get to override completely the likelihood of something unexpected happening.** The magician breaks the virtual wall that separates the stage from the audience when interacting with spectators, and this opens an infinite world of random possibilities.

Every kind of performer should know the particular conditions that apply to them. It is their responsibility to prepare their rehearsal pit as close to reality as they can manage.

Audience Management

We might wonder why sometimes magicians have this urgent need to interact with their audience. In my opinion, the answer has to do with the senses we intend to fool.

The entire theatre will see their emotions channelled through the spectator that interacts with the magician. With all his senses, this person is attesting of what he sees, hears, feels, and even smells!

It may be worth reminding that these same spectators who participate in the effect, with all their senses alert, are alive, and they are a significant random factor to learn how to handle on stage.

We must learn to control spectators as best as possible, and experience has taught me that learning to read the signs of their body language makes things easier. People in the audience feel safe in their seats, but when one of them steps into the stage this person usually feels out of place, and he or she immediately tries to get used to the new surrounding habitat. In those moments, the spectator's body will be an inexhaustible source of signs that will allow you to know key aspects of his or her personality. My advice is that you learn to read those in order to take some advantage for the effect that you are about to perform.

On more than one occasion, among the comments received after finishing a show, I have been congratulated for choosing the right spectators for each effect. I am sure this compliment is familiar to you too. I genuinely believe that I did not know much about them at the election time in many cases. I possibly started to learn about them while they walked to the stage, or during the first moments by their side.

In the first thirty seconds of your guest on stage, you should know if a spectator will give you the reactions you need. You could prepare a couple of control questions or some gags that could serve to help you quickly identify this person's profile.

I am not saying that you should ignore the crowd's body language when you go hunting for your "victim". I am sure you have also seen spectators who hold on to their chair for fear of being chosen by the magician. We should never force a person who ostensibly refuses to help us. It will not be worth having a hard time on stage. The audience will suffer together with the spectator, and this will not favour our presentation.

Fortunately, we will not find many of these spectators. Most people know that magic is an interactive show. Typically, those who come to the theatre know that the possibility of being called to the stage always exist.

Good audience management will help us reduce the risks of spectators doing something unexpected that could lead to a magician's mistake.

The fear of failing

I think the risk we take when we only care about "not messing up" deserves special mention. Our attitude will not be the same as in those situations when we only focus on doing things right.

It is an excellent call to assess the risks that we are going to take. We should do this at home, before the performance and as part of the rehearsal.

Once on stage, our mind already has many things to focus on. It is appropriate that you do so in a positive way so that you can always convey an attitude of trust towards your audience. Whatever happens, we should always show convincing control over any situation.

Final reflections

Mistakes and failures are part of our lives and our work. Despite their existence, we should be able to sleep like a baby if we work and strive in our preparation as artists.

My intention with this book is to help you put a collection of ideas in order. I think it is unnecessary to duplicate all our props, only to have specific ways out covered in the script's possible turns. Plus, we can get great benefits from the analysis of the risks.

Taking the "juice" out of the mistakes and the failures consists of doing a "forensic analysis" of everything that happened. After the autopsy, we will increase our knowledge, and it will be in our hands to take actions on the matter.

With the end of this first chapter, it is time to reveal the treasure hidden in the "philosophy" of these pages: Preparing for unexpected **adversities or surprises is also part of a creative process.**

Experiences lived in limit situations will help us at future critical times, and these will cause moments of personal reflection so that such problems do not happen ever again. Our imagination will then take care of finding possible ways out to apply to come to our rescue.

The secret, my friend, is that there will be a high possibility of creating new effects, previously unimaginable. You may be able to find original presentations, and you may even end up forcing some of your "rescue" outs if they turn out to be better than the initial effect.

Rehearsing Your Mistakes is a creative process where imagination, technique and experience come together to rescue the magician in distress.

"What the caterpillar calls the end, the rest of the world calls a butterfly."

– Lao Tse

...

..

.

Perhaps you are one of those readers who may be saying right now: Stop! I am already in the middle of a mistake, and I have not had time to get a life-saver ready! Help!

Well, dear friend, if you do not want to have to acknowledge your mistake to the audience, I hope that you have in your pocket some of what they call... real magic, also known as...

Improvisation!

2. Improvisation

"I have learned that people will forget what you said, people will forget what you did, but people will never forget how you made them feel." – Maya Angelou

We enjoy living comfortably in environments that we think we have under control. Starting with our breakfast ritual, we all have a daily routine for almost everything. We tend to do things the same way every day, from the moment when we jump out of bed until we go back to sleep at night.

However, we bump into unavoidable days when some things which are not part of the original script happen. Then, those things force us to improvise. When that happens, we feel more tired than usual at the end of those days. It is because that day we were forced to think a little, or perhaps a little bit more than usual, to move on with our day.

We control the routine situations as automatons, without any thinking. But as rational beings, we also can create new behaviours when we face new problems as they happen. The same thing applies when we perform on a stage. We usually try to follow a pre-established script, but some situations may demand forgetting about it. Whether we do it well or bad is already another topic, and although natural talent is essential, we can indeed improve with some training.

We call improvisation to **the spontaneous response to new and unexpected situations but under structured circumstances.** It is a way to get carried away but under certain control.

The audience can perceive the difference between acting on a role and "living the situation" through improvisation. The audience's reaction, therefore, will also be different.

Every person who steps on a stage in front of a group of spectators automatically becomes an actor. Dancers, jugglers, clowns, magicians... and even people from the audience who volunteer to assist on stage become actors. Acting is, above all, the art of the moment. Success lies in transmitting that you always live things for the first time, by showing natural reactions at every moment of the performance.

To further understand the power of improvisation, let us reflect on what happens when a magician picks a person from the audience to help on stage. This person steps into the scene without knowing what he or she needs to say or needs to do. Not everyone will respond the same way to that situation. The audience will enjoy more with someone who naturally and spontaneously re-emphasises what happens on stage, rather than with a person who puts endless barriers or blocks the performance.

Children often show greater naturalness than adults on stage when their help is required. Why? Shouldn't an adult know better than a child how to behave? Shouldn't an adult have further knowledge to interact? Well, dear friends, it is precisely in education where we can find the cause of inhibition to be carried away, to unfold naturally.

Education in our society teaches many things, but it is also a destructive process of the talent we are born with.

When we are kids, we do not try to control the future or to look good. Kids do not care about those things, and they simply observe. This is what allows them to be spontaneous.

Such is the power of improvisation that there is a theatrical genre based only on the improvisation of the actors. Shorts sketches or even complete plays are improvised in front of the audience by dedicated experts in the art of "improv".

Keith Johnstone, the great British-Canadian theatre director, is considered the father of improv theatre, part of which are the Theatresports, where two teams of actors compete on scenes based on the suggestions the audience gives them.

In the improv theatre, the main premise is not to analyse each situation before responding, but to let yourself be carried away by the first thought that crosses your mind. To be a good improviser, you must know how to inhibit the ability to analyse or select ideas.

Thinking is something we do all the time. To think is to establish quick connections that produce images in our minds. We do it effortlessly and without any intention. What really wears us down is having to make a selection out of all those images (ideas) to decide what to do, to discard all but one of the pictures. The longer time we spend selecting ideas, the less natural we will look, and the audience will perceive us as bad improvisers.

Improvisation is a resource that every performer (magician, dancer, clown, public speaker...) should have to some extent. Thanks to improvisation, we release our innate creativity. Simultaneously, it helps us develop a complete character; one that is more originally ours and more authentically unique.

Screenplay and Improvisation

As good professional magicians, we are supposed to have all the details of our show under control. Still, there are always things that could go out of the script: a spectator that does not collaborate, a mistake of an assistant, a device failure, a slip of the magician himself... the list can be endless.

What if we toss the script from the very start?

This is a fascinating and quite recurring topic of debate within the magical community. Many magicians are fervent advocates of the show's complete "scripting", while others prefer to put themselves in the hands of improvisation.

In my opinion, I believe that even if we have a natural talent for improvisation, we should not play with the results of our work by counting only on being inspired on the day of the show. An improvisation overdose has the power to ruin shows badly if we are not improvisation experts.

However, I also think that becoming stubbornly strict with the script does not immunise towards unexpected events, and it blocks crucial opportunities to achieve memorable and unique moments. Interacting with your audience can lead you to unimaginable situations with tremendous rewards.

Recently, I went to the first public performance of a good friend. After the show, we had dinner together, and we had the chance to share some thoughts. My friend told me that he was a little disappointed because he had interrupted the show too many times, as he had gone blank. He confessed that he had prepared a script with more than forty pages for his performance, which was only a forty-minute show! That night he had to acknowledge that he could not follow his own script on many parts.

My friend's story's silver lining is that you should not prepare an overly complicated script if you cannot follow it. My friend had invested six months in writing his act, but I never knew how much time he had invested in rehearsal. Clearly, not enough.

It does not matter if you spent a long time preparing your own script. Do not make the mistake of believing you will always remember everything. You should spend almost twice as much time rehearsing it. I am not the one inventing the wheel here, but it is something that some of the best presentation experts, like Steve Jobs or Scott Harrison, agree on.

A script's existence marks the way to go, but we must be flexible and keep an open mind. If the times comes, it will always be better to improvise than to stand still trying to remember the next lines.

Suppose we come across a situation that lays out of the script. Be cool. It does not have to be always a negative thing; sometimes, certain unexpected situations have the power of adding extra points to our presentation. Our experience will give us the confidence to play along and to improvise without taking unreasonable risks. Thus, we will take advantage of the spectators who attempt to trick us, we will turn unique situations into gags, and we will be playing with our audience and making the show of that day unique. And all this, not only without sweating but while enjoying the experience of improvising.

Risks and Memorable Moments

I think it is important to remind that **the audience is not silly**, and in most of the occasions we improvise, our spectators will notice.

If we do not do our improvisation right, we can quickly ruin an unfavourable situation even more. It is better to cut and to move on to something else rather than to continue stirring in some quicksand in which we could sink completely.

So, by now, you may be wondering: is it worth the risk? The answer will depend on each person, their ability to improvise and the situation itself.

If we do it right, spectators will rate it even above the original script. It is a big reward. It will create a special relationship between the artist and his audience, and they will go home with the special feeling of having witnessed a unique show that will endure in his memory. That is priceless.

At the 2010 National Magic Congress, held in La Coruña, a wildly unexpected situation could have ruined the show, but the opposite happened. The Rosalía de Castro theatre was full of magicians attending the congress to see the gala starred by many world-wide awarded magicians. Still, the big star of the night did not happen to be one of the performers, but a female spectator.

In these galas, where the spectators are magicians, there is usually special evident complicity between the performers and the audience. These performances are always full of gags and jokes that generate great laughter in the hall seats.

But that night in La Coruña, the unexpected event occurred with the laughter of a spectator. That laughter stood out from the rest because of its high volume, duration, and tone. It was an incomparable laugh, and it broke the pace of the performances mercilessly. The performers had to wait for the woman to stop laughing so that they could continue. That day, the great Norbert Ferré saw how that event ruined the "timing" of his ball manipulation entirely. It had never happened to him before. Norbert did not think twice. He immediately learned how to make the most out of the woman's laughter, and he integrated her into his gags. The whole theatre laughed to tears that night. We all gave great value to the improvisation of this giant of magic, and we left with the feeling of having witnessed something unique that night.

Learning to improvise

When we perform on a stage, our brain works at a thousand revolutions per second. Performing also means that we are taking care of everything the audience sees and everything they do not see. We go ahead preparing effects secretly, and at all times, we keep a transmission line open with the audience to convey the right emotions. This happens when we follow the established script, and we feel confident.

An unexpected situation immediately makes us feel under pressure. We feel undecided, untrusted. This is fear of the unknown, although many folks find more elegant linguistic figures such as cold feet, swollen tongue, or butterflies in their stomachs. You can name it the cheesiest way you like, but it is true that to improvise with confidence, we must break that tension.

When we improvise, either by desire or obligation, there is no script and, in a way, we are about to walk the tightrope. **Learning to**

improvise is learning to think. Our brain is continuously making connections at full speed. Our experience will give us confidence with the choice, but we must be aware of everything around us to get it right. Let's be flexible; let's lose all personal inhibition, and let's never stop transmitting.

Be aware of your environment

The time spent in recognising the environment is never wasted time. This could be a guideline from a general who wants to conquer a territory. Our conquest will be the stage.

To improvise with confidence, first, we must acquire a profound degree of awareness of the world around us. In other words, be awake!

In a way, acting and performing mean being in a specific trance state. We are focused on our character and everything around us. All our senses are alert. Reacting fast could represent the key to success.

Many professions require a similar trance state to perform better. Think of football players, for example. During a match, they need to be aware of a thousand things: the ball, the teammates, the opponent players, the referee, etc. But they do so in a state of maximum concentration that helps them act very quickly. They do not stop to analyse which direction the ball comes from, whether it is spinning too much or just a little bit, whether it is too windy or too hot... They simply "know" what they need to do, and they do it.

A little exercise: close your eyes (yes, you can be awake with your eyes closed too) and try to answer these questions: what colour is your T-shirt today? What kind of shoes are you wearing? Could you isolate and recognise the different noises in the room? (Hey! Do not fall asleep now!) Who was the last person you looked into the eyes? You were mesmerised, I am sure of it. What would you eat right now? Can you feel its smell?

Well, I would bet that after that little exercise, you have paused for a snack or a nap. I would not blame you. I hope that at least you have assimilated the concept of perceiving everything around us.

Humans are "multisensory" beings. From a young age, our learning through the world comes through our senses. Why do they put "Do Not Touch" signs in shops and museums? Quite simple, we all tend to play with things to have a better understanding. We always want to use all our senses to understand and increase our knowledge.

The key to real relaxation is the ability to focus on each sensation one by one, separately. If we open our senses and keep them in a state of alertness, we will be aware of everything around us.

A reasonable degree of awareness of the environment will also help to keep anxiety away from us. Without stress, there will be no mental blockage, and we will be in better shape to react to unexpected events.

In this "trance" state the number of mental connections we make is much higher. We will know what we need to do all the time. You might even choose to get out of the script yourself. You will feel like you "know" what you have to do.

Listen, look, feel, smell.

Losing personal inhibitions

To improvise we must let go and lose the personal inhibitions we bring from the "factory". We cannot afford to let shame play a nasty trick when we are dealing with a new situation on stage.

Every time my aunt Myrian watches me perform; she repeats the same remark: "I am amazed at how you completely become someone else on stage". For me, that remark is indeed a great compliment and a little win.

The performer (magician, dancer, clown...), whenever on stage, should always play a character. If we allow our character to possess us, our personal inhibitions will stop existing.

Here is a small game for you. Build a simple mask with paper and scissors. It could be the mask of any animal you can think of (a cat, for example). Then, still without wearing it, go in front of a mirror and try to behave as if you were a feline. Then, repeat the performance in front of the mirror but now with the mask on. Have you noticed any difference between the two versions? How did you feel?

It is possible that wearing the mask helped us to "get into" the character. Perhaps, you even got some inspiration from it. I bet your performance with the mask on has been more convincing than the one without it. Right? This proves that "getting into" the character helps us to free ourselves.

To get "possessed" by the character, it is not necessary to wear a mask. For many artists, costume and makeup have the same purpose. Any trick or help we come up with to get more "into" the character and let go can be valid.

We can also learn to let go through teamwork. By working side-by-side with other colleagues or with assistants, we could develop the confidence to take creative risks with a familiar environment's initial comforting safety. This will awaken a creative potential within us that for many, is undoubtedly still unknown.

Now, my friend, let me suggest a simple exercise of creativity to play with your body and your senses: how many ways can you come up with to say "hello" to someone in front of you? Wait, this time you'd better not use your imaginary friend. Take the first person you have nearby and play this little game with him or her. Start with your head, your hand, your eyebrows, your lips, your eyes... You will discover amazing things, I promise.

When we are children, we all play to pretend to be things or people within our universe ("playroom"). We play sailors, robots, Indians and cowboys, and of course, we also play parenting.

By playing these roles, we learn to use our bodies as a natural way of expression. As kids, we emphasise aspects of the characters that have created the biggest impression on us, whether in real or imaginative experiences. Kids do not follow any scripts when they get carried away to represent a role in the best possible way.

We achieve some harmony between the fantasy world and the world around us through this type of games. Is this not what magicians do at the end of the day? Remember, the stage is our "playroom". We set the rules there.

Never stop transmitting

Four elements are involved in all communications among people, which in turn are potential sources for indicators that could reveal if something went wrong:

- Words

- The voice

- The expressions of the face

- Body language

Words are the best communication channel. We use them to transmit messages in full detail. When talking, it is relatively easy to control the words we use, and we can always vary our speech on the fly. However, words do not reveal more emotions than the voice, the face and the body language.

Everything that influences speech is essential for the correct transmission of the message. The pauses with their right duration, the repetition of exclamations ("Ah! Oh!" ...), and the use of unfinished words can give clues about the authenticity of what we say.

The most critical vocal sign is the tone of the voice. When we are under the influence of an emotional disturbance, our tone inevitably rises. This will not be easy to hide.

Words often mask true feelings (emotions), but we can reinforce what we say through body language, which adds greater confidence to the message.

An excellent quote from Saint Jerome comes to my mind: **"The face is the mirror of the mind, and without a word, it reveals the secrets of the heart"**.

As performers, we could use those words to remind us that we should never lose eye contact with our audience. If we are improvising on a stage, it is probably because something has not gone as we had expected. We are in a limit situation, and we have to be able to get out of it. If the audience loses eye contact with us, the transmission of emotions will be lost, revealing that something is wrong.

Our body language must be consistent with the emotions we want to convey. The difficulty lies in the many expressions being on the edge of the conscious.

The expressions that can give us away vary with each person. If we tend to illustrate our words with many gestures, but suddenly we change the pattern, this will reveal that something has happened that has affected us emotionally. It is also quite common to rub or to scratch ourselves to reveal anxiety or insecurity.

I advise you to learn how to identify these expressions to know how to play with the emotions that your body transmits. A good starting point could be to start by reading some books about body language (highly recommended are the publications of Paul Ekman or Allan Pease). All of us can convey thoughts and ideas with pantomime, without the need for words, but for the artist, it is a must to learn to communicate with others through body language.

When we were kids, in our "playroom" we never had all the necessary resources to play sailors at sea, or astronauts travelling through space, etc. So we used our own body and whatever was around us to communicate our message. It was clear who our character was and our mission.

We must be the first ones to believe in what we are doing on stage so that our audience can understand the scene. This means, to some extent, engaging into a self-deception. That is the way to go, but I would like to point out that this has nothing to do with the essay published by Manu Montes about the so-named "theory of self-conviction" of spectators. As a side note, I also recommend reading about it to understand better how people's minds work when they experience magical effects.

It is essential to have a good mental image of what we want to convey to our audience. It becomes necessary to achieve an excellent inner perception of the invisible objects we use (shape, weight, texture, etc.) to be more convincing when transmitting our message. We must always promote the spectators' self-conviction (yes, now the one explained by Manu Montes). Since they will not question our body language, they will assume it and interpret it in their own way.

This time, the exercise I suggest you try is to represent a few actions only with pantomime. Try different approaches, exaggerate, get deeply into the character, etc. In short: play along.

Examples:

1- Tie your shoelaces
2- Hand out cards
3- Brush your teeth
4- Eat spaghetti
5- Crack an egg
6- Shuffle a deck of cards
7- Open an umbrella in the rain
8- Drop a heavy ball
9- Use a magic wand
10- Toss some magical dust

Status

Actors who train in the improv genre learn to use the concept of "status" from the early beginning. Comprehending this concept can come in handy when it comes to performing.

An actor's status on stage can be a confusing term unless understood as something one does to control people or be controlled by others.

In our daily lives, all people interact while we try to maintain a status. Every inflexion or movement implies a status; no action is casual.

If we want any scene to look natural on stage, the status of each person or "players" involved must be present.

We will talk about an actor or "player" of high status if that is a person who tries to be controlling and attempts to grab the attention. We will talk about a low-status actor or "player" if a person tries to be submissive or even go unnoticed.

The body language, the space each person occupies, and the on-stage conversations will reveal to the audience the status of the "players" on stage.

To understand this concept a little better, I would like you to look back and remember a teacher you adored, another one you did not like at all, and perhaps also one teacher that you considered a "poor man".

The "poor man" was probably a teacher who had trouble getting some respect from the students and showed quite a lot of insecurity. He would often seem uneasy and even out of place. He was undoubtedly a low-status person.

For sure, the teacher you remember who played some kind of high status liked to have his students under tight control, and perhaps he walked down the street as if he were the owner of each tile. Maybe, he would use piercing glances, and he would even ignore specific questions.

On the other hand, the teacher you keep good memories of was indeed a nice guy who did not need to raise his voice to get discipline, and maybe you could even say all the students loved him. That was a teacher who knew how to change his status with excellent skills. He would raise or lower his status as required by each situation.

Like teachers, when we jump on a stage, we stand in front of an audience that will evaluate us. With our body language and our words, we reveal a status which not always have to be the same during every performance. The audience loves witnessing how status transactions happen. These scenes are highly entertaining, and they often even end in funny situations.

You, better than anyone, should know what kind of status your character needs. But keep in mind that as soon as more people (helpers, spectators, etc.) share the stage with you, the status of each of these "players" will influence the development of the scene (performance).

The pleasure that students feel when they do pranks at school is because they manage to lower the teacher's status. Jokes and gags are mere tools to lower the status of other people. That is why it is essential to know how to change oneself's status to perform well in any situation. If a spectator on stage understands the scene as a competition, we have the risk of being torn apart. Instead, if the volunteers understand it as a game, they will show a cooperative attitude and enjoy their time on stage. It is amazing how great talent lives hidden in people whose appearance is entirely "normal". Let's not underestimate anyone's power of destruction.

Although on these pages we are talking about your character's status when you are performing, I would also like to point out that from the moment we are born, we all have a status by default. We all play with it during our lives. For instance, when someone takes a group photo, people pose and show some status that may not be real. Some people become the clown; others take a more boring attitude, etc. We can observe very different results in the "stolen" photos when people do not know that they are being photographed.

If you want your audience to like you, you must switch your status with your spectators during the performance. Think about what two friends would do. They both would care about making the other feel good, helping each other raise or lower their status.

When you tell a bad joke on stage, you may do it to laugh at yourself. This lowers your status, and it raises the crowd's one. The audience will help you get your status back up when people give you a round of applause again.

This principle of "status switching" (now I go down, now you go up) is used in most comedies. A comedian is an actor who lowers his status or someone else's.

In the comic strips, you often see these status transactions between the first and the last vignettes. The characters interact with each other while they change their postures. And why is it funny? Because of the unexpected twist in the status change of the character(s).

When someone's status gets snatched from a remarkably high level, we usually do not feel sorry. If an old man falls, we will run to his help as quickly as we can. But if instead of an old man, we see someone powerful, like a king, missing a step, many people will find it very funny.

Let's examine the act that made Voronin, the genius magician, famous: The scene starts with Voronin's characters walking into the stage in a very posh way, with a distinctly high status. The audience is looking silently at a guy that must be a great magician, proud and very smart dressed. Then, during the act, this guy suffers from different accidents. Things do not go the way they should, and the audience laughs at the "suffering" of the almighty magician. Voronin's status is continuously going up and down along the act. Each "failure" lowers the status and causes laughter. He then tries to recompose himself to return to a high status (by putting on medals, by maintaining a severe expression, etc.). However, after some brief moments, he is one more time snatched away when something goes wrong again.

The lesson here is that when a high-status persona is shattered, the whole audience feels pleasure, as they experience the feeling of having climbed up a step to a higher status.

If you do not learn how to make the right status switches on stage, you are in danger of not empathizing with your audience. The spectators will see you as a rival they have to beat, and, of course, they will experience great pleasure if you are shattered in front of them.

Spontaneity

Many times, throughout this chapter, I have been referring to spontaneity on stage. Maybe you think you are not a spontaneous person and wonder whether that fact will never let you learn how to improvise well. Before we move on to the next chapter, I will show you that it is possible to turn non-imaginative people into imaginative ones in a matter of seconds. After all, spontaneity and imagination are closely related.

Your case is not exceptional. Do not worry. Most schools encourage children to be non-imaginative. Their teachers censor imaginative children by default.

According to Torrance, "many children with little imagination have gone through quite severe efforts to eliminate fantasy at a very young age. They're afraid of thinking".

Perhaps we could say that children are immature adults, but we could flip this opinion over, and we could look at the adults as atrophied children.

Let's remember that improvising is choosing the first idea that goes through our minds. Being spontaneous is a behaviour pretty close to this idea too.

Schiller said that non-creative individuals "are ashamed of the momentary madness that the true creators experience. Any idea could be quite insignificant and extremely adventurous if you look at it just by itself. But it could become important if you link it to the idea that follows; perhaps, together with other ideas that could seem equally absurd, it could provide a beneficial connection".

Some people may think that the artist is the one who makes the most elegant choices after excluding and eliminating ideas. As we will see later on this book, in the chapter about creativity, the creative's success relies upon the number of ideas one has or carries out.

Do you think that using your imagination requires a bit of effort? Does it take a lot of concentration to put an image in your mind? Come on, let's try a little experiment.

Read the following lines:

"John Smith is driving a bus down a great avenue on a rainy day. Suddenly, someone tells him to hit the brake..."

I could have drawn these lines from a novel, but that is not the case. I have written them myself because they are the first thing that came to mind in order to show you that you have used your imagination when reading those two sentences. I am sure of it.

Have you imagined the bus being full of people or empty? Was that vehicle of any specific colour in your mind? Was the driver wearing a cap? What about a uniform? Could you tell me if John was clean-shaven? Was there traffic around the bus? Why do you think someone told the driver to slow down?

Do not tell me. You have answers to all those questions, and it did not take long for you to come up with them. You did not think about them; you just knew the answers because you have seen it in your mind. You imagined all that yourself. Did you notice a great effort? I am sure that was not the case, right?

Your imagination has created all the images that have passed through your mind. Not only do images pass through your mind when you read a novel, but ideas also flow in the same way when you are on stage, you just have to grab one of them and see where it takes you. Ideas generate automatically, like lightning in your brain.

Many people block their imagination because they are afraid of not being original enough. We base our concept of originality on things that did not exist before. When we improvise, we should not worry about being original. The audience enjoys when someone is direct, and they laugh with pleasure when the idea is very obvious.

As spectators, we all have a cute little monkey in our head waiting to see something that he recognizes so that he can start clapping with great joy.

Trying to look smart by looking for the most "original" idea is a big blocker, and this subtracts points from our performance.

To be spontaneous and a good improviser, you must accept situations as they happen. Accept these "offers", and you will be rewarded with amazing adventures. Here is a connection with the status concept, since a low-status character tends to accept, while a high-status character tends to block. By taking the "offer" of an unexpected situation, the audience understands that your status just went down, they will like you a bit more, and they will celebrate when you get your status back up.

We could consider everything a spectator spontaneously does on stage as "offers". Then, each of these "offers" could be accepted or blocked by the artist.

Good improvisers can make us believe that they are not improvising at all and that everything had already been scripted in advance. This is because they accept all the "offers" that are made to them.

Once you learn to accept any "offers", accidents will no longer interrupt the performance. Everything will flow continuously, and the audience will enjoy more than with the scenes that contain blockages or barriers. Those always go against fun.

Let's do a little experiment:

We should organize a party. To everything I am about to suggest, you need to say "yes" and, please, add something else, basically the first thing you can think of....

- Let's have a party!
- Yes! And let's buy balloons!
- Yes! And.......! (It is your turn)
- Yes! And let's get some mojitos!!
- Yes! And.......! (It is your turn)
- Yes! And let's dance the conga!!

It does not matter what you came up with for our party. The crazier, the better. Well done!

Now, let's keep the "yes" but let's replace the "and" with "but".

- Let's have a party!

- Yes! But we have little money!
- Yes! But.......! (It is your turn)
- Yes! But it's cold!
- Yes! But......! (It is your turn)
- Yes! But beer is expensive!

All right, to which one of the two parties would you like to go?

Don't you agree with me that the first party seems like more fun? Just think about it for a moment. You got excited, didn't you? Now, try to put yourself on your audience shoes when they watch one of your shows. The same principle applies here. Not putting barriers to "offers", even if they are totally out of the script, could become the gateway to a new exciting world of adventure, entertainment and fun.

Reading about improvisation and spontaneity will not make us better improvisers nor more spontaneous people. That is true. But at least we may stop going in the opposite direction. A good lesson we learned today if we became aware that **we were fighting against our own imagination whenever we tried to be imaginative**.

On stage, we could invent the whole world around us, even for the volunteer from the audience sharing the scene with us. We are magicians, and we have the power to equip our volunteer with a new character. It is in our hands to give this person a unique role in the performance. Just, my friend, do not be too evil, we know what you are capable of.

If the idea of signing up for an improv theatre workshop has been crossing your mind, but you have not finished deciding, let me tell you one thing: It is a great idea! Go for it! I guarantee you will develop a lot of new skills, and at the same time, you will have the time of your life.

Often, business executives also attend small theatre groups. Sometimes, they are even encouraged by their "crazy" companies! There, they learn to have better control over their bodies and their senses to learn how to express emotions and to communicate better with others. As performers, we have a much more important reason for signing up if we want to be good professionals in show business. Do not hesitate. Look for a course or a workshop and sign up.

...

..

.

The lessons from improvised performances or ways out deserve a chapter aside. The situations that go out of the script should only require improvisation the first time they happen. In the past, we could have handled them spontaneously in the right or the wrong way, but we should always take the lesson into account during our preparation to...

forecast the future!

3. Forecasting the Future

"When a voyager begins a journey, he prepares his ship, decides upon his course and sets sail. What else can he do? But he cannot know the outcome – what storms may arise, what new lands he may find, or whether or not he will return. That is destiny, and you must accept it. Never think you can escape destiny." – Edward Rutherfurd

Most of us, illusionists, sooner or later, we end up defining ourselves within a category: escapologists, card magicians, dove manipulators, etc. The truth is that we all share one, although not all of us show it in public: mentalism. When we are rehearsing, we are all trying to forecast the future.

It is no secret for the audience that we spend long hours practising our techniques to acquire flawless executions. They do not know that we also strive to anticipate what will happen in our show to succeed no matter what.

No, you do not need to call any fortune teller's line. You may leave that for your science experiments on the paranormal. You would not make much progress, and they would charge you a real fortune! Forecasting the future should be part of your rehearsal.

Suppose that during our performance, something happens that goes beyond the script. In that case, we will always find ourselves more

51

comfortable, and even more prepared, if we had already contemplated the possibility of that situation happening.

Imagine you have invited some friends to have dinner at your place tonight. Perhaps, you want to show off your cooking skills, but you may not remember your grandmother's recipe very well. The result may not look the way you expect, or your star dish may not be to the taste of the picky girlfriend of one of your friends, or one of your guests may have an allergy to an ingredient that you are not aware of… Then, when you are about to suggest that you all meet in a nearby restaurant, you stop to think for a few moments, and you discover that you may be able to prepare yourself for some of those situations. After all, you could probably manage to become a great host. If any unexpected events arise, for sure your guests will recognise the skills of a great host who is ready for adversity.

When developing an idea during the planning of our show, the script is always linear at first. But from that point, we should start to analyse what could go wrong (understanding by "going wrong" to everything lying outside the original script). The preparation of possible drifts or detours of that linearity will result in something that we could call a new script with "branching".

The Attitude

One of the well-known Murphy's laws states that if we drop a toast, it will always fall with the jam-side down. Murphy must have been a very pessimistic guy because he clung to believe that anything that could go wrong would end up going wrong.

If you think in the same way as Murphy, I do not know why you bother reading this book, because it is highly possible that this is a very bad one... Well, I would better not go that way.

I am reluctant to believe that there is someone out there who is really convinced that Murphy's laws control anyone's daily life. If that were the case, many people would not even get out of bed, others would never have dreams, nobody would risk a thing on new ventures, and nobody would ever show their creativity to others.

Any new project we develop, no matter if it is a personal or a professional one, is going to require a strong will from us to move forward. Adversity will turn up sooner or later. We need to face it.

The key is **to analyse all the possibilities and never to abandon an optimistic-realistic attitude.** As in the lyrics of the song written by *Ashford and Simpson*, let me tell you that there is "no mountain big enough, no valley deep enough...".

Once, Walt Disney was asked about his remarkable skills to create new characters with new stories and new fantasy worlds. The answer was short but straight forward: "if you can dream, you can do it". All progress in any area is achieved by breaking the barrier of the impossible, by reaching a little further from where it is believed that it can be reached.

Mickey Mouse's father was **aware of the limits and obstacles, but he made a significant effort to find new paths that took him way further than others.**

A magician's creative process works under the same premise. Being aware of all possibilities will always be beneficial for us and our magic.

Some creative magicians start from the end of an effect, and they build the routine backwards. They start from a dream, and they make progress by collecting breadcrumbs, like Tom Thumb, to return to the real world, where the physics laws rule and people who unfortunately believe in Murphy's laws live.

Wait, do not lose focus. The creative process of a magical effect from the beginning or the end is a different topic than the one I want to tell you about, and although it is very fascinating, it must be told on another day.

The creative process which I would like us to reflect on is one that begins with the possibility of a mistake, a flaw or an unexpected situation happening. It is the creative process of organizing the rescue of the magician in distress.

Therefore, before setting off to search for possible complicated situations in which we could find ourselves, it can be an excellent idea to prepare ourselves with the right attitude.

Always remember that when you show a positive attitude, you have enthusiasm. And when you are excited, you can get the best in you. Thus, you are the best version of yourself.

Instead, when you lose your temper, you lose the best you have. The difference between the big and the mediocre may lie only in the way we feel.

Now that you know what kind of attitude we should have, here are the rest of the tools we need.

What do I need to forecast the future?

In football, there is a term named "game vision" or just "vision". It applies to both coaches and players, and the more they have, the better they know what they need to do every moment, especially in the complicated ones. It is a skill that is directly related to imagination and experience.

Game Vision = Imagination + Experience

As performers, we have our "game vision" too. We do not use it only while we are playing our "match" on stage. We also use it to prepare the performance to forecast situations that could happen later during the show.

So, we could also say that in magic, the "game vision" is made of the sum of imagination and experience.

Imagination

Many people may think that forecasting the future is extremely hard. Their excuse is often the lack of experience. However, I believe it is more of a problem about not using their imagination enough. If this is your case, do not worry. You can fix it. And if you also have no experience, you'd better pay attention, as your imagination will be your only asset to develop the vision.

Our imagination works like a muscle. We need to exercise it to get good feats. **Our minds need a daily workout to stimulate the imagination as much as possible**.

Have you noticed the little children? They are freaks! They can develop an exceptional imagination thanks to their games in which they simulate situations that they would like to live. They do not just pretend to play in fantasy worlds, but also in the real world around them. They play adult roles to buy and sell stuff, teach at the school, have tea with friends, and endless etcetera.

Are you getting where I want you to go? You must play!

Here, my friend, are some ideas that can help you exercise your imagination:

- Try to remember what you dreamed last night. It does not have to be very accurate. It is enough if you have some mental flashes of your dream. Then, take a blank paper and draw the scene of your dream. Finally, add some details that could look good in your drawing, even if they were not present in your imagination.

- Relax with some soft music, close your eyes and try to imagine yourself in different situations: a sunset on the beach, a dip under a waterfall in the middle of a forest, a cup of hot chocolate next to a fireplace, a night walk around your favourite place under the full moon... Try to imagine the smells, the sounds, the flavours, the presence of whatever is around you...

- Write funny things that inanimate objects would say if they could talk to you. Try to guess what they would say to complain about their task, or to thank you for the use you make of them...

- Get together with some friends and play "telling a story", each one of you adding a sentence in your turn. Then, see how far you go.

- ...

There are countless methods to develop your imagination, but you must forget about the hustle and bust of everyday life for all of them. Relax and let your mind fly.

In case you consider yourself too serious and too adult to try this kind of thing, you will not make much progress with your imagination. Reading books like The Little Prince or The Neverending Story could help you bring out the child you carry inside.

Perhaps, when you start practising with these light exercises to work out your imagination, you will probably take refuge in the typical excuse "I'm not very inspired today". Hey! Do not be anxious and go slowly. Being constant is very important here, as it builds up every day and over time, you will see good results. I promise.

Think about those odd weeks when you crack your wires, and you decide to get your body in shape. From the beginning, you already know that you are not going to lift huge weights during the first week, nor are you going to finish many kilometres when you go for a run. I bet you do not try to find any excuse on the lack of inspiration then. No, you will probably find your justification in the stew, the drinks, and those long TV evenings.

When it comes to exercising the mind, we must also be regular in our exercising. Encouraging imagination is a process that needs to go beyond a couple of afternoons. The good news is that it is a lot of fun, you are not going to sweat, you do not need to feel hungry, and you could share this work out with your friends and family. After all, these are games.

If you need a little push to convince those around you to play with you, get them Dixit. This boardgame is super fun, it has no age limit, and it aims to develop the players' imagination. It is a brilliant boardgame. I am not making this up. Dixit was awarded "Game of the Year" in 2009 by the Germans (*Essen Spiel des Jahres)*, and these guys know a lot about these things. No, I do not take any commission, but I will be happy to play a few rounds with you.

Television and the internet are great evening fillers, but at the same time, they block our imagination and ultimately our creativity. Watch out and make responsible use of them.

By the way, if all you do is watching magic videos, either to learn or as a way to seek inspiration, you are fooling yourself a great deal. In a video, we get it all done, and it is more difficult to add a singular perception of our own. When we watch a magic clip or a dvd, we get knowledge in a passive way; instead, we need to use our imagination when reading a book. The author guides us with his descriptions, but we are the ones who need to process the mental images.

Mariano Vilches first recommends intellectual assimilation of the effect described in the book, before rushing to practice it with coins, cards, etc.

Experience

The famous "experience" attributed to the artists who control the stage exceptionally is also a useful resource for the process of forecasting the future, although more limited than imagination.

It can be extremely dangerous to perform an effect that has already gone wrong once if we have not found a remedy in case it happens again. Most likely, our confidence will not be that high, we will be more nervous, and we will be giving a warm welcome not only to new mistakes but also to the same situation again without any emergency way out. We must not stumble twice on the same stone. In other words, we must not let the same dog bite us twice.

For many years, in my show, I have performed the effect of finding spectators' cards by pinning them with a sword. The audience never suspects that the presentation includes a blade until the moment they see it, but the story I tell, and the atmosphere created for the act justify the sword's production.

I had been immensely proud of my act until a fateful night when it went wrong. The unimaginable thing happened. For reasons that I still ignore to this day, when I went to look for the sword, I found it broken. Then, I immediately froze because I had no way out of it. What could I do? I am sorry. The end of the story is not very interesting. I apologised nervously to the confused audience, and they never knew what had gone wrong. But they surely knew something had gone wrong, as I stopped the presentation and moved on to the next routine.

That night, I was not able to fall asleep at all. I felt terrible because of my mistake on the show. I could not let things like that happen again, and I was determined to find a way out. Before long, thanks to the presentation of the effect itself, I was able to find it.

In my act, I never said that I was going to find the cards by pinning them with the sword. I only explained the impossible challenge of getting a hold of the cards before they touched the ground. Then, I had the idea of adding a hat to the performance. And if I ditched it to the floor to indicate the area where I wanted the cards to be thrown into the air, I could get a completely valid way out.

Since then, I have never found the sword broken again. But if that situation ever happens again, the audience will see a dramatic ending, as they will think that I will have failed as they will see all the cards on the floor and none in my hands (nor in the sword). Then, it will come the right time for the emergency plan: with rehearsed theatricality, I will show the audience that not all the cards touched the ground, by producing from the wings of the hat... the cards of the spectators!

Of course, this emergency plan is only one way out that is not as impressive as the sword's original effect, but it does fit perfectly as a rescue plan. It is the "fire exit" that allows me to stay alive. Once I got this situation under control, I went back to perform this effect many times, and certainly with greater confidence.

So far, I have never needed to present the emergency finale with the hat, but at least I have a plan until I come up with a better one. With this plan in my "tool belt", my performance is more robust.

The more you perform, the more personal experiences you will have, the more variety of spectators will help you with the effects, and the more unexpected events will happen. Isn't that exciting? Your experience will increase, and your performing skills will be more significant.

Ascanio's words come to my mind: **"Magic is a practical art that we learn in front of the audience"**.

If we always wait for a situation to happen before investing some time to find a remedy, we will never be mastering the stage. Unfortunately, we have not been given one life to rehearse and another one to perform. Then, we must go a little further from everything we know to fight the unexpected.

The smartest attitude is to try to use our experiences combined with our imagination to find alternative plans in case we face some possible limit situations.

Other's Experiences

The years of performing on stage are important, but we cannot expect to live all the possible situations for ourselves.

Once, someone told me: **"anyone who wants to do magic must also see a lot of magic"**. There is great truth in that statement. We can learn a lot about how other artists deal with adversity, about how they interact with complicated assistants, and how they move on to succeed with their show.

Years ago, after watching the movie Forrest Gump, I kept thinking about certain scenes for a while. In the movie, everyone felt sorry for the main character played by Tom Hanks, and in a way, I did not feel like Forrest was that miserable. He was involved in plenty of different experiences: he had been to the Vietnam war, he had become a table tennis champion, he had kissed the prettiest girl in high school, he had travelled to space, he had succeeded fishing for prawns, and an endless list of other things. What a life!

By far, we cannot get to have such a variety of experiences in life, and the same thing applies to our life on a stage. For this reason, I recommend the healthy habit of talking about your experience with unexpected situations and mistakes with colleagues. By sharing experiences, we can not only find new solutions but also gain those experiences for ourselves.

Debbie McGee, the lovely wife and great assistant of Paul Daniels, revealed in an interview that she was a little lost with the cameras when she started working on television, not knowing which one she had to face every time. That problem did not last long, because after watching Carol Roy, whom she admired very much, she perceived the technique she used to deal with the same problem. Every time Carol Roy lost sight of the camera activated by the director, she would make an elegant spin on herself, look for the new position of the little red light, and continue to smile directly at the viewers at home.

In the magic world, we are all creative to a greater or lesser extent. You will find that for the same problem, many different solutions have been found. They all deserve our respect. There does not have to be a universal better solution. A solution that could be the most valid one for you may not suit another magician in his presentation.

Now, dear friend, I would like you to take a moment to think about what happens when we see a colleague making a mistake on stage. Sadly, the most common thing is that we dare to criticise him badly, without realising that we could find ourselves in the same situation any day. It is not our show, and for sure we lack much information to be entitled to question our colleague. Let's be gentle and nice with the artist. Let's put ourselves in his shoes and suffer with him. If we do this, we will add that experience to our "baggage" and later on, we could reflect on a rescue plan in case we find ourselves in trouble facing the same situation.

Risk Assessment

Once we have identified a bunch of possible deviations of the script, we no longer hold a valid excuse to rate them as unexpected. It is in our hands to do something about them. Don't you agree?

Remember that an essential part of this creative process is to face these risks with the right attitude.

Eventually, you may come across more situations that could potentially ruin your routine than you could have expected in the beginning. But keep calm, my friend. Do not be overwhelmed. Maybe, worrying about them is not worthy, nor spending time to try to avoid them or to look for ways out. Let's see how we can increase the quality of the time that we will spend rehearsing the new branches of the script.

After identifying the risks, we need to think a little about them and make a proper assessment. The result will tell us if it is worth taking the risk, or whether we should work towards minimising or even suppressing it.

Here is a method to help you assess the risks of your performance and your show:

61

Make a table with all the "unwanted" situations that you have identified. Proceed by assigning a numerical value based on the **likelihood of occurrence** of each case; and then, set a second numerical value based on the **impact** that each event would have on the effect or the presentation.

You can use the scale you want for these numerical values. I am used to writing values between 1 and 5 for both grades to keep it simple.

Impact on the Effect/Routine

1. None

2. Minimum

3. Medium / Depends on others

4. Important

5. Catastrophic

Likelihood of Occurrence

1. Highly unlikely

2. Unlikely

3. Likely

4. Very likely

5. It happens for sure

If you wonder why I am not using the word probability, it is because I am faithful to my high school math teacher. That man made a great effort to teach me that the range of probability values always goes between 0 and 1. But well, that is a story that, although interesting, should be told another day.

Next, we will see an example of how to make a proper risk assessment for a simple routine of card magic: a force with a revelation using a second deal and a final prediction.

> ➤ **The Predestined Card** *(Learning example)*

Effect: *A freely chosen card (only in appearance) by a lay assistant is lost in a deck which then, gets mixed. The magician produces the card when the assistant tells him to stop dealing.*

As a finale, that same card matches the prediction made at the beginning by the magician.

Method: *We start with the deck prepared with the card that we want to force in the last position of the deck (bottom-1).*

At the beginning of the routine, we give the assistant an envelope with a prediction. Then, we pull out the deck, and we force the card with the classic force.

We will pretend that we are losing the card somewhere in the middle when we are actually placing it on top of the deck (top-1).

Finally, we will be doing second deals until the assistant says stop. At this point, we will reveal that the next card is the chosen one.

But the effect does not end there. We still have the prediction that, of course, matches the chosen card for the finale.

Now, let's say that we want to do this small routine to one of our cousins. That cousin is a little bit "special". We know that he always wants to touch everything and that he is still very sceptical when we do magic. Besides, he will not be alone. His girlfriend, who does not care about magic, will be with him.

I did not want to get very excited by coming up with strange events or strange situations. So, leaving extra-terrestrial abductions aside, this could be a possible risk table and my **personal** assessment of occurrence and impact according to the scales presented above.

	Situation	Likelihood	Impact
A	The deck gets messy before the effect starts and we misplace the top card	3	5
B	We forgot giving the prediction to the audience	1	3
C	We failed with the force	3	5
D	The assistant loses the card himself, and we lose control over it	4	2
E	We failed with the second deal	3	3
F	The assistant does not remember his card	2	4
G	The assistant loses the prediction	1	5
H	The prediction envelope is empty	2	5

I am sure you could come up with many other extra possible unexpected situations that could affect the development of the routine. Good job! Look at you, getting your mind to work already! That is great. But as this is only a learning example, let's proceed with the above table for now.

I want to emphasize that this assessment is very personal, and it may be possible that you feel like assigning different values to the situations in the table. Well, that is fine. But let me explain a little bit the criteria that I have followed to give the scores.

a) We misplaced the top card that we wanted to force
   I know my cousin well. And I may not be able to keep him away from the cards. And he may mix the deck and mess it up before we begin with the routine. This would ruin the effect of the prediction that I hand out at the beginning of the performance.

b) We forgot to give the prediction to the audience
   This is something that I am quite positive it will not happen as it is the very beginning of the routine, and I am rehearsing

it quite a lot. Anyway, were this to happen, I could always stick to the cards routine and skip the prediction part.

c) We messed up with the force
If we find a way of being aware of this mistake, we could always follow a different script branch. Otherwise, it would be terrible as this mistake ensures the complete failure of the final prediction.

d) The assistant loses the card himself, and we lose control over the position of the card
I know my cousin well. I am sure he will try to lose the card himself. No problem. If this happens, I will go straight to the end and reveal the prediction.

e) We failed with the second deal
Catastrophic result. We managed to lose the card ourselves. We would have to go straight to the prediction, but we would need to find a reason to explain all the dealing.

f) The assistant does not remember his card
My cousin usually pays a lot of attention, so not very likely to happen. However, if he forgets, I could not rely on his girlfriend remembering either. It will not ruin the effect, and I will not reach the desired magic climax. Maybe this could even make them feel bad. Who knows...?

g) The assistant loses the envelope with the prediction
This is very unlikely to happen too. Remember, I am not contemplating alien abductions today... although I admit that the impact would be terrible.

h) The envelope with the prediction turns out to be empty
Unlikely with all the preparation we have been through. It would be a perfect anti-climax situation after the first effect of the routine. We would definitely be nominated for the "dumbest magician of the year".

If you look closely, you will see that while I have been evaluating the impact of each situation, I have also been throwing some possible alternative plans. That is also going to happen to you when you try to assess the impact score. The likelihood of these "temporary" contingency plans usually lowers the impact score.

But wait, do not rush to try to find some alternative plans to reduce the impact. Sometimes this can be challenging, and you might want to spend your time on something else first.

Once we have the assessment of each situation ready with the likelihood of occurrence and impact, it is time to place them both on a new table. This table will be the final risk assessment.

Now, let's start from the following reference table:

Likelihood of Occurrence

I \ O	1	2	3	4	5
1	Low	Low	Low	Low	Low
2	Low	Low	Medium	Medium	Medium
3	Low	Medium	Medium	High	Extreme
4	Medium	Medium	High	Extreme	Extreme
5	Medium	Medium	Extreme	Extreme	Extreme

Thus, the 8 situations in our example get their risk assessment.

Situation	Risk
The deck gets messy before it starts	Extreme
We forgot to give the prediction to the assistant	Low
We failed with the force	Extreme
My cousin loses the card himself, and we lose control over it	Medium
We failed with the second deal	Medium
The assistant does not remember his card	Medium
The assistant loses the prediction	Medium
The prediction envelope is empty	Medium

Often, the result of the risk assessment may be a surprise for some situations. How can all these situations be classified as Medium Risk? Still, some of them are highly unlikely to happen, right?

My advice is not to touch anything for now. From experience, I can say that we are always more accurate in estimating the impact than the likelihood of occurrence.

The first situations we should get to work on as soon as possible are those assessed as Extreme Risk or High Risk. In my opinion, a routine that holds such risks should never be presented to the audience. Depending on whether you have some plans B or ways out ready, you could vary the impact and likelihood score in the table. This will lower all the potential risk you agree to have for the performance.

We should not underestimate the situations that represent a Medium Risk. However, we should not be overwhelmed either. We could use the likelihood score to prioritise working on them. But remember that if one of these situations happens, and you still do not have a way out, you will feel quite stupid for a long time.

I suggest you use this method to analyse some of your favourite routines. If you are surprised by the results, will you tell me?

We are the creators of our own presentations. We do know our limits and virtues, and along with a hint of experience, we should be quite accurate with this assessment.

Remember that if you want to increase your level of confidence with a more objective risk assessment, you will need the help of a colleague you can trust.

Rescue Plans

Reducing risks can be a very complicated task or even close to an impossible one. There are factors beyond our reach that also come into account and that we cannot influence.

We can work on reducing the risk of making a mistake when we force the card in our example, either by using a different forcing technique or by investing more hours in practising "the classic force". Either way, I find it quite hard for this situation's risk score to be any lower than Medium Risk. We are going to need an emergency plan for this one, a rescue plan.

It would be ideal if the rescue plan could allow you to continue with the routine as if nothing had happened. Unfortunately, this rescue plan will most often force a change in the structure of the effect or the presentation.

If we see ourselves in this situation where we just missed to force the right card, a possible plan could be to discard that first card with some sort of excuse and try forcing it again but with a different technique. That would not alter the effect a bit. On the contrary, if we accept to continue with the wrong card (badly forced or freely chosen by the assistant), we know that either we vary the routine or mister failure is waiting for us at the end. Other alternative contingency plans could be performing another effect with that card or finishing the performance with the second deal production and leaving the prediction effect for later.

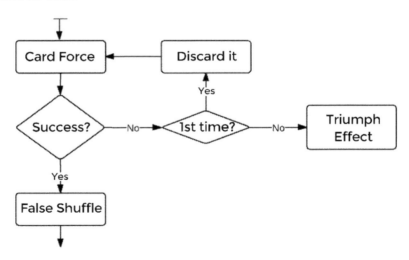

The diagrams known as "decision trees" help us visualize the rescue plans and their influence on our routine. In this example you can follow that if I fail with the force of the card the first time, I will discard it with an excuse and I will try it again, most likely with a different technique. Then, if I happen to fail with the force again, I will move on with a different routine, in this example a simple "triumph" effect, which does not need a forced card.

Don't worry. There is not a universal answer to every problem you face. You need to find out which way out could work best with your presentation and your circumstances and only then, follow that path. Remember to keep your spirits up!

Try not to put sticks on your own wheels. When looking for rescue plans, we will also come across the unavoidable environmental restrictions in addition to the conditions we have already imposed ourselves. Therefore, I personally do not like the effects in which the magician anticipates what will happen with all the details explained. The more things we tell the audience, the more we are going to limit ourselves in case we need to use our contingency plans. If a magician anticipates that he will reveal a card under certain conditions, then if any of them show a flaw, the effect will fail. Keep that in mind.

The issue with the matches

One of the first problems I got when I was starting to perform had to do with the matches I was using in my show. They did not always light up well when I pulled them from the scrapers in my jacket. Luckily, it was not a serious mistake since the spectators were not expecting a lit match to be produced from the inside of my clothes. However, it was a detail that spoiled the rhythm of the effect and the presentation.

This was the path I followed to find the right solution for me:

Solution 1: Never use matches; always use a lighter.

It was much more magical for me lighting a match than just pulling a lighter out of my pocket in my presentation. This solution could reduce the risk significantly, but I was not convinced. Besides, the lighter could also fail and break the rhythm.

Solution 2: Use a lighter as a backup fire.

Again, a reasonable solution, but it would be a little strange to remove a lighter immediately if the match did not ignite. The audience could wonder why I did not go straight to pull out the lighter.

Solution 3: Load a bunch of backup matches into the scrapers.

With this solution, I risked turning the act into a match manipulation routine. And perhaps, in the end, spectators might never see any lit matches at all. It would be totally ridiculous.

Solution 4: Scratch the matches manually.

What about pulling a match and then going for the box to scratch it? This would make very little sense. It would make more sense to draw the match straight out from the box.

Solution 5: Scratch the match magically.

Removing a lit match from the clothes is a magical detail that adds a bonus to the act. If I pull out the match and it is not lit, the least that could be expected from me is that I could magically light it up. What does it take to light a match? A scratch. And to make it a magic ignition? Creativity.

I finally went for solution 5. I had the idea of trimming the side strips from a matchbox. I attached one of them to the surface of a stage prop with some adhesive. As a backup, I also attached the other strip to the back of a chair that I always had on stage. Lastly, I also decided to always carry a lighter in a body holder as the final contingency plan. (By the way, Pedro Aragonés shows in his lecture how to make a great "all-in-one" holder for lighters and matches. That is a "must-see" for all magicians.)

Shortly after integrating this problem's solution in my show, I saw Juan Mayoral performing his act with the coat hanger. That day, his jacket's scraper did not work, and he pulled out a match with no light. I drew a smile of complicity on my face when I saw him continue with the presentation by successfully scratching the match on his shoe.

Mayoral's solution to the same problem with the matches had gone in the same direction as mine: in movies and cartoons, matches are easily lit on shoe soles, on wooden poles and even on three-day beards. The audience believes that in a fantasy world, it is entirely feasible to light a match in those conditions, and Juan Mayoral's solution perfectly met that belief. Now, I invite you, my friend, to try to light a match on the sole of your shoe, on a rough wall or a little shaved beard... in most cases, it will not work. Remember, you will need a little creativity to make it possible.

Over the years, I have witnessed dozens of contingency plans from fellow magicians for the matches problem. **There is not a universal solution better than the others.** Each magician ends up finding the right one for his presentation. And that, folks, is the beauty of the little details. In the end, those details define our work and ourselves.

Final Reflections

Sometimes we will struggle to find a solution for a problem, but other days we will find many ways out. That is life.

Ascanio said he only knew how to perform one or two routines perfectly. This statement coming from a genius like him could indeed draw our attention, but Ascanio did not believe in absolute perfection in the execution of a routine. According to him, once a magician comes to master the technique required by an effect and is comfortable with his presentation, he begins a journey that may never end. It consists of a search for perfection that, in contrast to how fast we may have come to feel comfortable with an effect and master its technique, it will be a slow process towards the unknown. It takes many (or way too many) years to polish details of a routine to make it perfect. Let's be restless and curious, let's explore alternatives and maybe, one day, we will find a lovely treasure.

As I know that you, my friend, are a good performer, you have probably already mastered all the techniques that your presentation requires. Then, it is time to apply the theory of this chapter: analyse what could go wrong, study if you could avoid those situations and if that is not the case, find rescue plans.

Remember that the less stuff we leave to chance, the more under our control we will have our performance.

> ...
>
> ..
>
> .

In this chapter, we have learned that with our personal experiences, together with those from our colleagues and with our imagination, we could prepare ourselves for future situations and mistakes. We will be able to forecast disastrous events and find solutions for them. And perhaps, if we are lucky, we may discover a solution that will make the effect more extraordinary.

But is it possible that we get to the point of craving something to go wrong so we can proudly show our genius rescue plan? Shall we aim for the mistake and the flaw?

4. The Search for the Mistake

"The strong man makes his events, the weak submits to those imposed upon him by destiny." – Alfred Victor de Vigny

Throughout history, many magicians have used false flaws on their shows. These are situations that are forced by themselves. These do not happen by chance. First, the artist makes the spectators believe that an effect has gone wrong, and then shows a way out that knocks them out.

Not until recently, the great majority of society began to consume performing arts and movies so frequently. This explains why nowadays some people hold a certain level of expectations at the theatre, at the cinema or in front of the television. The audience is no longer amazed by the simple fact that the images on a screen came to life, nor by a stage actor who learned a long script by heart. Spectators set a quality bar that goes up as they become more "experts" by consuming more shows.

I am sure that years ago you watched a movie that had just been released, which at the time you thought was quite good. Unfortunately, when you watched it again a few years later, you no longer held the same opinion, right? You may even find it hard to believe how there was a day you could get to enjoy it that much with that obvious story, or with those old special effects. Can you see what happened there? In the last few years, you have seen so many movies that your perspective and demand level have changed.

Why are movies such as Inception or The Sixth Sense so successful? In these productions, the ending changes the whole plot. It shows you in just a few seconds that for two hours you have been watching a different movie than the one you thought you were watching. You have been "tricked", and you like it. That final surprise transforms a regular movie into a good film that you will recommend to your friends.

The same thing happens in magic shows. As the years go by, spectators become more experts about our performing art, and they become more demanding. It is not enough for them watching the magician make feather flowers appear from his sleeve, nor watching a transformation of silks inside a change bag. The minimum level had always been that the magician did not fail. However, people take that for granted on any good magician. Today, we need to offer much more. We need to entertain with our presentations, to enchant with our words and choreography, and of course, to create emotions. And the more intense these are, the better!

When a magician simulates a failure in his presentation, he is shaking the audience's most basic expectations. It is not that the mistake makes them question whether the artist is a good or a lousy magician. If the magic effect fails, could it be that perhaps the performer is not even a magician?

Simulating a failure in magic can be a tremendously powerful weapon that ensures intense emotions. But that weapon handled without control can be catastrophic. Therefore, if you want to be a good magician, you should learn how to use it properly.

Use cases

A fake mistake allows the magician a broad range of possibilities. It could be useful to divert the audience's attention away from a secret move, put the audience on the side of the magician, make the character look more human, establish a thick atmosphere of drama, and achieve a higher final climax or for countless other purposes.

In the same way that it is advisable to master a little touch of psychology to perform a card force successfully; searching for the mistakes also requires a little bit of it. It is essential that the spectators understand the situation well, and that the final effect justifies or completely amends the former mistake.

We can use certain flaws as gags within the presentation. However, the audience must understand those as such. They need to produce laughter, and the audience should be able to differentiate the gag from the magic effect without any doubt.

Magicians who specialize in performing for kids know that one way to attract the young audience's attention is by pretending that things go wrong. Through intermediate failures, we could show the great difficulty of doing something magical. When we finally get it, the audience will cheer us up for the remarkable feat we have just accomplished.

Artificial failures make us more human and bring us closer to the audience. Remember the concept of **status** on stage and how status transfers work among the players. The stereotype of a magician is a high-status player, and therefore, the audience is on guard by default. They do not want to be fooled by a "smart ass". A mistake will help us lower our status.

We will get our audience to laugh with our desperate attempts to do magic, if every time we try something, we encounter a new problem. Maybe, the audience will eventually take our side, they will encourage us, and when we finally get the magical effect successfully done, they will feel part of it. We could even say that a presentation with artificial failures can minimize or even suppress the conflict with the audience, explained by the great Pepe Carroll.

But most certainly, the incredible power of artificial mistakes lies in the ability to increase the climax of an effect. For spectators, a failure is something unexpected; a sudden surprise they did not imagine possible in the magician's script. This concentrates all the attention of the audience on the artist. They are expecting the artist to do something to fix the mess. A good way out from a failure (forced or casual) may generate more applause than if the situation had been "expected" by the audience. Thus, one simple effect that fixes the issue could become sublime magic.

I would like to stop here for a few moments to illustrate the power of that statement with an example. Let's take a classic of card magic, one of those "sandwich" effects in which the spectator's card appears between another two cards.

* Do you not know how to make a sandwich? In most of the presentations of this sort of effect, the spectator picks a card and perhaps, he even signs it. Then, the card gets lost it in the deck. With the help of two other cards, the magician will then try to find the spectator's card. After some magic moves, the spectator will be amazed by how the chosen card appears between the magician's two unique cards.

But what if the card that has been "sandwiched" by the magician is not the chosen card? The spectators will be disappointed, as they were really expecting to see magic, and somehow, they were hoping that the magician's cards would locate the signed card.

Now, let's review Aldo Colombini's fantastic effect, "Sherlock vs Moriarty".

> ➤ **Sherlock vs Moriarty** *(Learning Example)*

When introducing this routine, Aldo presents his two "police" cards as Sherlock Holmes and Doctor Watson, the famous detectives from Sir Arthur Conan Doyle's novels. Then, the assistant selects a card that plays the role of the evil Professor Moriarty. Once signed, the card gets randomly lost somewhere in the deck.

Once nobody knows where the villain is hiding, it is time for the bold detectives to come on stage. When the magician loses these two cards (facing up) in the deck to find the assistant's card, he only mentions that Sherlock and Watson will go *"looking for clues"*.

After a few moments and some magic moves, the two police cards show up (face up), but "guarding" a face-down card between them. At this point in the story, the spectator is already taking for granted that the face-down card is most likely the signed one.

When the time of revealing the "sandwich" comes, Aldo flips the middle card saying... *"and Sherlock and Watson have found... the 6 of diamonds (e.g.)"*. By then, the spectator is most likely showing a poker face and rushing to say that the 6 of diamonds was not the right card. Aldo immediately says *"Elemental dear helper! I never said this was your card, but it could be a clue that could lead us to it"*.

With this collection of events, a new suspense atmosphere has been created in which the spectator is not entirely convinced about whether the magician has failed... Then, Aldo quickly explains that the card that has been found indicates the position in the deck where the spectator's card was last seen. The assistant, still not very convinced, proceeds to count the cards one by one, and in position number six... Whack! That is where the signed card is hiding!

+   +   +

Indeed, master Aldo Colombini plays with the spectator's mind. The routine is built in such a way that, although at no time it is said that the signed card will appear between the two cards of the magician, the spectators create that idea in their head (and more rightly, if that is not the first time they see a "sandwich" effect). As Manu Montes would say, the spectators convince themselves based on their knowledge and the subliminal information that the magician has been delivering in small doses.

Would you not say this is great magic? With a simple presentation spiced with some small subtleties and special care of the words, we could trigger "evil" ideas in the spectator's mind. In this sample case, Aldo chose to make the assistant believe that the effect had failed. However, **such a failure turned out to be nothing more than a ploy to increase the climax of the performance.**

It is also this kind of effects that get the best comments in the magic congresses. As Juan Tamariz explains in his *Magic Way*, the audience gets carried away by the magician throughout the routine. We make them trust us, "beware of that rock on the trail", "come here that the landscape is prettier", "follow me slowly because here we could fall down"... until we finally say "now you go ahead, you are safe, and you are going to love it"...and thud! The audience slams badly into a wall, pushed by the devastating force of the magical effect. Luckily, the hit causes no pain but big emotion. The people in the audience enjoy the smart "deception", and they laugh at the unexpected situation.

Dangers and a piece of advice

It is not easy to get such situations in a magical effect. If we do not build the routine well, we have the risk of reaching an **anti-climax**. The audience will still think that the effect has failed, and the solution will have been nothing more than an unsuccessful attempt to fix the outcome. No botch jobs, please!

If we intend to make the audience believe that the mistake is not part of the script, our acting skills must be pretty good. Remember that spectators are not fools and that if they detect from the beginning that the failure is scripted, they may not be that surprised when you later fix it.

You will have many spectators who are regulars of magic shows. And perhaps, some of them had already detected that the technique of simulated failure is a ploy of illusionists. The advice I presented in the improv chapter can also be given here to convey that we are living these mistakes for the first time.

Exaggerated use of artificial failures could potentially develop into an anti-climax situation. A comedy performance with too many repetitions of the same mistake over and over again could easily become really tedious.

It is not convenient that all the effects that we present in our show have this artificial failure. Depending on the atmosphere we want to achieve, the mess could give a hint of originality or drama and increase the expectation of a specific routine within our recital. If the simulated mistake becomes the common denominator of all our effects, it will lose its strength.

Good taste and delicacy are also important when choosing what could go wrong. If you make the audience suffer too much, later they may not enjoy discovering that everything had been scripted. They could take it as a bad joke. Are you one of those who need to show blood to prove that you have genuinely screwed things up?

The Magic Way, which Juan Tamariz guides his audience on, is filled with false clues about the effects whose existence the spectators should neither see nor suspect. The artificial mistake is a type of fake clue, extremely dangerous for the unexperienced magician, but it has excellent potential for adding a bonus impact on the effect.

Why does it work so well?

The human mind works in an extraordinary way. Little by little, psychologists help us to understand it better. With the artificial failure, we have been taking our audience to the point of disappointment. They had expectations for our show as little as they could be, and they have not been met. But luckily, they do not suspect about our evil intentions. We wanted them temporarily in that state of mind, so later we could get a more significant reaction to the grand finale.

In our daily lives, we often happen to create too big expectations ourselves: a birthday party, a trip with friends, a date with a special someone, etc. When the time for the truth comes, if those expectations are not fully met, we will always be somehow disappointed. I am sure it has happened to you too.

We love surprises. When things go beyond our expectations, it triggers a feeling of happiness and almost unexplainable emotion inside us. It is the same thing we want to achieve with our magic. They are the so-called memorable moments.

Memorable moments

I think I will always remember my final Electronics exam at university. The semester had been quite hard, and I had put a lot of effort and enthusiasm into that subject. It was not my first year at uni. I was quite aware that even if I was happy about an exam, I could always have misread a statement, messed up with the initial approach to a problem, and I could end up with my joy vanishing like a dream. Despite that fact, I thought the exam had gone well for me, and in the following days, I started to believe that I could get a good grade.

A couple of weeks later, without knowing the test's grade yet, I was about to spend a few days on the beach with my friends when I received a message in my phone from one of them. Chopi: "I'm sorry, man. Electronics' grades are out. The teacher is showing the tests tomorrow afternoon".

I almost started crying. All my efforts during the course, all the sacrifices, the hope after the exam, everything had been useless. It was not fair! The next morning my friends would leave for the beach, while it would be my turn to visit the teacher and find out about my mistakes in the exam.

But that was not the end of the story. Only five minutes later, I received a second message from my friend Chopi: "Well, you'll have to go to the review only if you are interested in visiting the teacher. You've got a 6.8. Congratulations".

The rush of joy I felt then I could not describe with words because they simply do not exist. First, my expectations were high. Then, they had gone down completely, and a new surprise event had beaten all my possible dreams. My heart was literally jumping inside! I felt like I was on a roller coaster of emotions!

Of course, then, I immediately dialled Chopi's number to yell at him for making me suffer like that. The next day we went to the beach together, and we laughed about the whole prank.

I will always remember this story because **it was different. It had an unexpected but happy ending**. I did not suspect at any time that they were taking the mickey out of me. In the first message, they did not tell me that I had failed. It was an inferred but not explicit idea in the statement. It was customary in my university that the failed grades were not appearing on the list, and that was why I thought my friend was not telling me my grade in his first message. Chopi knew of my great hope over the long-awaited grade because I had said to him that I had even dreamed about it!

You may be one of those who think it is impossible to compare such emotion from real life with the feelings produced with a magical effect. If so, let me tell you that you are wrong. Aren't there dreams, books or movies that get your heart pumping? Then, in the same way that a spectator feels emotions and cries with certain scenes in the cinema, we can produce feelings just as strong with our performances.

At times, human beings have an excellent ability to inhibit particular reasoning and not distinguish reality from fiction. Every day, we dive into fantasy worlds when we read a novel, when we watch TV, when we go to the theatre or the cinema, or when we get mesmerized by the lottery poster. We put ourselves in the shoes of the protagonists and feel everything they feel. Prickly goosebumps break out across our arms and stomachs with the great war speeches, we get touched with the family scenes, and we mourn the loss of the loved ones that we have just met in these fantasy worlds.

However, the emotions created within these worlds can persist in our real world. Or have we never been afraid to go to bed after watching a horror movie?

With these experiences, we are aware that we go into an unreal world, but we like it. It takes the stress out of our daily worries, it is entertaining, and it reminds us of the dreams that remain to be fulfilled.

Several years ago, I was practising a small effect of mentalism that I wanted to include in my show. It was a test of the living and dead. And the first person I tried it on was Sara, my assistant at the time. She knew very well that it was a new effect, and as such, it was only a magician's trick. Despite this, she could not help crying like a little girl because of the emotions she felt. I admit I was a bit scared because I did not expect that. However, Sara reassured me that it was indeed a wonderful effect and that I had awakened some memories and emotions that were very intense but beautiful.

With this example, I hope I have shown you the potential that magicians have to create emotions too. We are artists perfectly capable of inducing ideas in the spectators' minds and of intentionally bringing them to the point of disappointment. We can make them believe that their journey through our fantasy world is suddenly over when, in fact, the real roller coaster is only about to begin.

Robert Houdin was the first to understand that every illusionist's mission is none other than the job of an actor who has the role of a magician. Therefore, as we are actors, we have the same power to arouse all kind of emotions in the audience. Be aware of it when preparing your presentation. If you can thrill your audience, they will remember you forever.

How to fail properly?

The temptation to cause your own mistakes may have grown as you have read this chapter. Before we continue, I want to remind you to be careful once again because playing with errors is comparable to playing with fire.

The search for the mistake may help you improve some of your routines. To find the right mistake you are looking for, were it to exist, you can use the method to forecast the future explained in chapter 3.

All unwanted situations you can think of will help you develop rescue plans that could potentially be new and different effects. The next step will be to ask yourself this question: are these rescue plans better than the original effect? If the answer is no, do not even think about it and strive to follow the original script with the peace of mind of having some ways out covered now.

If the answer is "yes", then your mission is to force that situation and find a way to infer into the minds of the spectators the idea that the effect genuinely fails. It is important, as otherwise, it will seem that everything is scripted, and you will not be able to boost their emotions.

Depending on your character and the presentation you are using, you may even be able to acknowledge the mistake explicitly. It may work well if you have a character who is a (voluntary or involuntary) witness of magic. If your character is a master of magic and admits a mistake, it will only be to amend it later and of course, in a significant way.

Involuntary witness characters or "victims" of magic are usually illusionists presenting comedy acts. The mistake is somehow in line with the character. Some well-known magicians who use this technique are Tina Lenert, Jaime Figueroa or Jandro.

A master magician who has great control of magic, such as Jeff McBride or David Copperfield, if he comes to admit a mistake, it will be so that later, there will be no doubt with the final climax that such a mistake had been intentional. With the presentation of a challenge, this magician manages to end the natural conflict with the spectators and gets them on their side.

I think we do not need to go for one of these two extreme roles because it could be easier not to measure well and get "burnt". In one case, you are in danger of not being credited for the miracle, and in the other one, the climax reached could not be enough to make the audience forget the mistake or reveal it as intentional.

The safest area is to move between the two characters: start the presentation with the role of a guy who witnesses magic; then, be an clear involuntary witness of the mistake, and end the performance by fixing the situation with a climax that proves that everything is under your absolute control. The audience will be aware of the status transfers that occur throughout the routine; they will get excited about you, encourage you, and be amazed by the final surprise.

Is there any magic effect that follow that plot? Of course, and here goes one of my favourites.

> **Any Card at Any (Page) Number** (Joshua Jay)

The magician begins the routine by revealing his passion for reading. He explains that in all books, countless wonderful secrets are hiding. After this introduction, the magician takes the opportunity to present the last magic book he has purchased. It contains the instructions for one of the classics of magic: "Any Card to Any Number", a wonderful but complicated routine.

In case someone in the audience has not heard about it, Joshua continues to explain what this effect is about. That makes the spectators crave to see it with their own eyes. Then, the magician notices his audience's desire, but he apologises by saying he still does not know how to do the effect. Right before the disappointment starts to sink in, Joshua offers to show them a version of his own he had been working on for some time.

The magician draws a deck and begins the performance, which seems to follow the expected script. A spectator chooses a card from the 52 possibilities. At the same time, another person picks a random number that will indicate the position in the deck where everyone will expect the card of the first spectator to appear later.

A surprise with great disappointment comes next. The card in the named position turns out to be a different card. Oh! The magician has failed!

Then, after a theatrical pause that builds up some suspense among the spectators, the magician (so far, a mere witness of the effect) comes to the rescue: "*Well, my friends, you may remember that in the beginning, I told you that I was going to perform my own version of the effect, not the classic one. I explained that books contained many exciting secrets... and besides, you could also find numbers in them, a different one for each page...* "

Then, the magician gets the audience's maximum attention when he reaches for the book, which had been set aside but in the spectators' view at all times. Now, it is time for the grand final climax. The page matching the number picked by the spectator is surprisingly hiding the selected card. Here you have an incredible miracle!!

What do you think? Isn't that wonderful? That same thought is what goes through the spectators' minds who feel great pleasure with the final surprise.

+   +   +

I want to thank Joshua Jay for creating this routine. The "Any Card to Any Number" is a powerful classic routine. Still, with the added intentional "failure" and the subsequent recovery of control with the final climax, the magic effect becomes a hammer.

Since 2009, when I attended Joshua Jay's lecture in Valongo (Portugal), I have included a version of this effect in my repertoire. I wanted to tell you about it in this chapter because I consider it the perfect effect that proves the search for the mistakes useful. It is a routine full of details that take the spectator along the Magic Way. And when it seems that it will be impossible to reach the destination, the magician comes to the rescue to catapult us to the most beautiful magic unimaginable rainbow.

If you know how Joshua Jay built this routine and apply the method to forecast the future of chapter 3, you will notice that it is very well shielded. The most "terrible" thing that could happen here would be ending with the classic version of "Any Card to Any Number". Isn't that great? Without a doubt, the dream situation for any routine. Thank you, Joshua, for this piece of art.

Rewards

In chapter 2, we already saw that if some good improvisation worked well for us, it could produce the so-called "memorable moments". These were enjoyed at the same time by the magician and the spectators. A well-constructed routine with an intentional failure can also create a "memorable moment", although this time only spectators perceive it this way.

Being able to artificially create some of these great moments in our show is a tremendous reward. The artist has no risk of having a heart attack, and this time no extra effort is required on stage in the way improvisation needs it. We will have everything under control, and we will enjoy the presentation even more.

In case we have some ruthless spectators, the mistake manages to get their full attention. We will have the whole audience focused on our next move.

The mistake has also made us more human, and the spectators will feel closer to us. We have managed to dissolve the conflict between the magician and the audience. We got them right where we wanted!

The final effect that we had previously planned is boosted after the artificial turn of the script. The climax becomes more intense, and our spectators enjoy it more.

In 2010, a journalist telephoned me about a charity event that was about to take place in my hometown, Palencia. It was a rather odd interview since the interviewer constantly forgot about the main topic with her questions. Despite my insistence, she made me talk about many other things. When they published the interview, they put this headline: " No art exists that demands more improvisation than magic." – *El Norte de Castilla, 24.03.2010*

The headline they had chosen had nothing to do with the charity event. The interview was worthless. They only put four cliché questions with a bunch of answers that I did not even remember to have given.

And then, there was the heading. Of all the things I had said in the interview, the reporter had kept that headline. She did not bother to put a context to it. She heard it, and she decided to use it to draw attention to the article. How unlucky!

My intention was only to explain that unlike other performing arts where the audience is just a passive spectator, in magic, the theatre's fourth wall is destroyed, and the audience participates in the performance. I wanted to imply that this fact triggers unique moments, which we could have never rehearsed.

Or maybe we could have rehearsed them? Aha! My reader friend let's keep it our secret. If our audience goes home with the feeling of having lived a few unique moments in our show, it will be our triumph. That is the great power of artificial failure. It may be improvisation for the audience, but for us, it will be part of the script that we will pretend to live for the first time. Let them think they have experienced something unique. It is worthy.

...

..

.

In this chapter, we have reflected on the power of simulated mistakes in our presentations. We have seen that we could decide to infer the idea of failure in the minds of the spectators, as in Aldo Colombini's routine, or to accompany the audience in that moment of disappointment, as in the Joshua Jay's effect, by acting as if we lived the mistake for the first time.

The search for the mistakes is a creative method for presenting a magical effect in which the audience sees that things do not go as they should, and the magician must come to the rescue.

We have learned that the mistakes could catapult our show toward success if we solve them well, or into a disaster if it blows up. Therefore, it is also convenient to learn to recognise the point where there will be no turning back...

The Point of No Return!

5. The Point of No Return

"There is no reason to punish yourself for not doing better. You did everything as best as you could. Release the past with love and be grateful for this new knowledge in your life." – Louise Hay

In the previous chapters, we talked about how we could deal with the mistakes on stage. We have been learning different techniques and tools that we could use, to minimise its likelihood of occurrence or its impact on the show. And in the last few pages, we saw that we could even use artificial failure to get stronger emotions in our audience.

But what happens when all our resources are not enough in the event of a failure? What happens when we cannot recover the audience from the state of disappointment where we have put them? Now, we have run out of plans, and not even a good improvisation could hide the mistake, we have not brought the alien tool that could erase the memory of our spectators... we are lost, aren't we? The answer is: Yes.

I am not kidding. The moment we run out of plans, no ways out, no inspiration to improvise... then, we will have reached the **point of no return.**

The moment a mistake happens on a stage, you become the paratrooper who just jumped into the air from the plane. However, you do not have a stack of folded fabric on your back; in your "backpack" all you carry is your knowledge, your script, your skills to improvise and your experience. You are already in the air, and the future is in your hands. You have some room to open the parachute, but only as long as you do not get to the point of no return.

From that moment on, it will be useless to keep trying anything, or making pointless quick excuses. We are going to be slammed and since we are going to fall, let's do it with dignity.

When did we get to that point? I can only tell you that when you reach it, you will know how to recognise it. You will feel it.

After so many lines and so many pieces of advice, you may think, my friend, that we are in the start position again: nervous and undecided with a problem in our face that will lead us to mess up an effect in public, to our failure. Well, it is not quite like that. If we have prepared ourselves as best as we could, at least we should not blame ourselves now.

Let's be elegant and fall in style. There are few options: let's try not to put much attention to the matter, let's pretend it is not that important, or let's apologise sincerely and make no more excuses. The less time we invest in it, the less importance we will give to the mistake, or at least that it will seem like that (which is all that matters). Anyone who can laugh at himself conveys to the audience an emotion that relaxes the tension that arises when they see the magician's mistake. That is the moment of recovery when the smart magician will take advantage to perform a routine to take control back over the show.

So, why have so many tips been served? Have we been wasting our time on all this thinking? Well, the goal is clear, to keep this point of no return as far as possible from us. The more prepared we are, the more unlikely we get to this point of no return.

I admit that I also like to tag these situations as a "point of no return" because I intend that they will never happen to me again. I never want to come back to them. We simply could not afford it. Not going back there should be our goal. It must be the point we cannot go back to. Sorry, I cannot help saying it again and again, so you understand how important this is.

I like the well-known quote that says "sometimes you win, other times you learn". Let's try to maintain an optimistic and realistic attitude despite the failure. We may have bad luck, but defeat should never be the end of our track. Let's learn from it.

Learning means assimilating that experience, analysing what went wrong and why we reached the point of no return. This reflection exercise is on a mission to incorporate into our "backpack" some additional tools, even if it is a last-minute lifesaver, to avoid returning to the same deadly dangerous situation.

I am sure you must have heard some random magician using these words: "Before I proceed with the effect, I'd like to warn you that I am still practising...". It may not be those exact words you have heard, but a similar version of them. By saying that, the magician believes that he has just laid a soft feather mattress in case something does not go well. Boo! Get lost!

If I hear someone saying those words, I immediately classify that person as someone with a lack of confidence, lack of preparation or lack of both at the same time. Nothing worth my interest. After hearing those words, I do not feel like looking at the effect any longer, unless that was only the magician's character in a role.

That magician was creating a self-deception by thinking that were a mistake to happen; that mattress of sympathy would be a lifesaver from feeling unwell or would prevent the audience from feeling disappointed. With those words at the beginning of his performance, the audience already started to feel that way. And all that achieved with the routine without even having been started!

If you think you need to announce a warning like that before your act, you are not ready yet. You need to spend more time with your rehearsal. Maybe, not in practising your techniques, but in the study of situations that could happen so you could have all the ways out covered and thus, you could gain some confidence.

Perhaps, you may want to justify that some situations could not be encountered during any practices. Okay, but the magician's rehearsal must also have a phase of analysis of many other factors, besides the effects.

Next, you will read about how you could reduce risks in your shows. I am aware that many different situations could happen to every artist. Many various factors could influence the development of a show, but here you will find some tips on some fairly common problems.

Risks Reduction

In the world of theatre, movies, television, etc. actors must worry only about playing their roles. How lucky! They do not need to squeeze their brains to write a script, they do not need to study what kind of lights are most suitable, nor will spend hours and hours looking for the best songs that will accompany them on stage and of course, they will not strive to prevent what could go wrong. With a couple of exceptions, all magicians tend to take care of all these things and many more themselves.

So, the day you stop feeling butterflies in your stomach before you go on stage, you will know it will be your time to quit. Even the most experienced illusionist can never be sure that everything will go flawlessly. This artist will feel comfortable on stage and have prepared countless tools and secret plans for situations that may go away from the script, but this performer is also aware that there will always be a minimal chance of failing.

The risk we take is directly related to the adrenaline that is simultaneously going through our body. Ah, the adrenaline! It is the "drug" that pushes us to perform in public and to show our magic; and I am sure that, just like me, you also feel a deep addiction to it.

Just as when you play with fire, you always have the possibility of harming yourself, the same thing could happen to us with mistakes. Did you know that firefighters wear cotton underpants under the fireproof uniforms to avoid the danger of the flames? The uniforms' reliability is very high, but just in case, fire professionals never hesitate to go a little more prepared with a minor extra effort.

In a magic performance, there is always a substantial number of potential dangers. Some of them are far from the artist's responsibility, and little or nothing could be done about them. But about the risks that the magician is personally responsible for, something could be done. These are things like insufficient preparation, way too much confidence, little motivation, inadequate mental state, not enough energy, stress, gimmicks in poor condition...

Little Preparation

Sometimes, we may encounter risks arising from insufficient preparation. If we make the mistake of presenting an effect without the right amount of rehearsal and practice hours, we will open a door to an infinite world of possible calamities.

There is no chance we will ever rehearse an act "too much". The more time we spend on the rehearsal, the better prepared we will be and the more unlikely we will fail.

It is possible that under certain circumstances, we find ourselves pushed to speed up the presentation of a new effect. If we are aware that the preparation time has not been enough, and yet we have no choice but to present it, let us be careful with our body language. If something secret from the audience goes wrong, we will transmit our doubts and possible negative emotions to the spectators, and we will be giving ourselves away.

Overconfidence and Little Motivation

In most cases, experience counts in our favour when it comes to predicting possible unscripted situations. However, it could also play against us by making us feel too confident and too relaxed in the face of danger. Do not let your guard down.

Overconfidence and lack of motivation go hand in hand when we repeat the same effects performance after performance. I will not discuss to Aristotle that excellence is achieved through repetition, but it will be challenging to keep it for a long time if we are unmotivated. And overconfidence could lead us to make mistakes.

Every magician should find a reason for personal motivation. Maybe we can remedy this problem if we include small new details in each performance. I do not want to say that you dare to completely change the whole routine that has always given you the best results. That would be a great risk, indeed. But perhaps, you could slightly vary some small details that are not very important in the end. These will help you transmit to your audience that you live things with the first time's intensity and enjoyment.

That strategy is commonly used by magicians who perform shows day after day since they encounter the problem of not having enough time to prepare new routines. And if they want to keep their contracts, their employers may demand a new show in the mid or long term.

You could also try to improvise with little things such as a gag or a conversation with your assistant or with someone from the audience. Remember, one of the keys to success for improv actors is always living events for the first time. Little improvised details have the power of getting your motivation back and staying connected to your performance with the right dose of confidence.

Inadequate Mental or Physical State. Stress and Lack of Energy

The first thing a magician presents on stage is his image. It does not matter how much make-up we wear. If we are tired or we have our head elsewhere, our performance will deteriorate.

Before artists, we are people, and we must take care of our health by living a healthy life.

We can achieve the right physical and mental state by playing sports or taking some vacations from time to time and having a life outside of magic.

I owe Juan Mayoral the best advice that a magician has ever given me. At his lecture in Santander, he stated: "**We can never be good performers, nor can we have an interesting personality, if we don't do in our life different things other than magic. Life has many wonderful things to enjoy and to learn from**". Magic must be a dressing of a life outside of it. That helps us when it comes to getting on stage and when creating our shows. Travel, practice sports, read novels, have friends outside of magic... LIVE A LIFE!

If we see that we need help to get into the right mental state, the best thing we could do is paying a visit to a psychologist. We should not be ashamed to go to these professionals because they are qualified people who will give us the best guidelines to recover our mental and physical health.

Think about the top-class athletes and how many years of their life they invest in working on the same task. They try to achieve perfection continuously under thousands of eyes, which is always a huge pressure. And that is their routine! All top-class athletes make use of psychologists, so they can manage to keep the right state of mind.

Tools and Gimmicks in Poor Condition

In our presentations, we use props and gadgets that should always be in the best condition, although sometimes we are too lazy to replace them or keep them under a mint condition. This is not only important for creating a good impression, but for ensuring that things will always work.

Some magicians do not like to use gimmicks, while others cannot live without them. I do not see anything wrong with using gimmicks as long as we never forget about studying the manual techniques. If we give ourselves the luxury of being gimmick-dependent, we will be at great risk. Gimmicks on their own are powerful, but when something goes wrong, or they simply break, only the manual technique can come to the rescue.

The manual technique alone can accomplish incredible things, but it has its limits (in the end, we have no superpowers. Right?). Together, gimmicks and technique, they make the most powerful toolset the magician can have. Gimmicks will allow us to do many wonders comfortably (in most cases), and technique will assure us that if something fails, we will not be lost yet.

Treat all your material carefully. It will last you longer. Be careful with your props when you rehearse, when you travel, and when you get your things ready on a venue.

At the venue, try to ensure that no one but you or your assistants touch your material. Do not allow that either before or after the show.

Check your tools, clothing, and shoes frequently. If you adopt a routine to do it before and after the performance, you will ensure that everything will always be in order and ready for use.

Fear of Failing and Self Confidence

Popular wisdom among magicians says that to succeed with a performance, the artist must go on stage "to eat the whole world up". These words carry the truth that the magician's attitude is not the same when he concentrates on doing things right as when his thoughts only haunt the idea of not failing.

We must not be afraid of failure, but we should be cautious.

When presenting a magical effect, we are walking the tight rope at many meters high and without any safety net below. We can equip ourselves with a parachute, but there will be a chance that it will not open in time and we will hit the ground.

Do not worry. I have not sided with Murphy's laws. I am just playing for a moment the role of the devil's advocate.

We can distinguish two types of fears that can affect us: the fear of failing at a specific time (in a card force, in a body load, etc.), and anxiety as an emotional state prior to the performance, the well-known stage fright.

The fear of failing at a specific moment can appear when the artist defines the moment itself as crucial, and one gives greater importance to the wrong action over executing it right. Some beginner artists externalise this fear when they close their eyes just before completing specific steps, such as some secret moves, which makes them look less natural and reveals that the "trick" lies there.

The attitude when facing crucial moments on stage is different on every magician. Some artists draw my attention when I notice that their fear of failing is reflected on their faces only once they have successfully overcome all the previous obstacles and want to be more careful with the ending. Instead of getting more and more confident during the performance, they become conservative when it comes to putting the icing on the cake.

To be among the best and get the biggest ovations from the audience, we must have the mindset "to eat the whole world up" from when we first set foot on the stage until we finish the performance. To reach the stars, we cannot cover all the way only with a ladder, the last rung will always be far away, and we will need some courage to jump.

In her performance in the 2003 Eurovision Contest, Singer Beth was a clear example of "failure for extreme cautiousness" on stage. For the first time in many years, a contestant from Spain attended the European song contest with a good song and a great voice with enough skills to win. In front of our screens for the big date, the Spanish audience saw how Beth started to gain confidence with the first stanzas while she looked relaxed on stage. When we were all already thinking that it was finally our year to win the festival, the moment of the most challenging part of the song arrived. It was when the singer had to reach a very high tone. What Beth had so many times proved right; she could not do it on that night. She chose not to raise the tone that much to avoid messing it up. The audience that had previously listened to the song many times clearly noticed that the singer was acting cautious, and we all immediately knew that once again, that year the award would not come to Spain. Beth's score was good, but not the best.

The psychological variable that has the most influence on artists' fears is self-confidence. A confident magician does not think about the consequences of a potential mistake. This performer only focuses on giving his best and on making the audience enjoy.

Years ago, a friend convinced me of the idea that we can only think positive. This idea refers to our minds not being prepared not to think of anything. When we focus on not failing, what is actually drawn in our head is the mistake. This is the pillar on which many psychological forces used by the best magicians in the world rely. When you tell someone "don't think of a red car", the spectator's mind will picture it anyway, even if later that person is led to think of a different colour.

Some tips to improve self-confidence for our show:

1- Let's be focused at all times. Good skills to concentrate and a solid pre-performance routine will help you achieve this. The routine will be solid if it is not affected by the results or by previous mistakes: playing a video game on your mobile phone, singing a song, doing a short yoga routine, playing with a deck of cards... Anything could work. And it does not have to be related to magic. Whatever it is, it should allow you to enter a state with the right concentration to go on stage. (Someday it will surely be worth writing a book about the funny pre-performance routines of many artists...)

2- Once at the theatre, we should never do an analysis of things that could go wrong in our routine. It should only be done previously at home, as part of our rehearsal. Before going on stage, we must set ourselves with the right attitude and focus only on success.

   Suppose we see that any of the environment's conditions could affect us when we arrive at the theatre. In that case, it will be worth considering using a "substitute" routine that we are confident performing. Then, we could leave the "starter" one on the bench until another day.

3- During our performance, let's focus on every step. Let's give importance to the great things we can do, and let's not be bothered by the result. The result should not surprise or relieve us since it should be the typically expected outcome. Aren't we great magicians? Remember that the audience will notice our feelings and our inner energy. Do not worry about the final result of the performance. This one will only be important once the show finishes.

4- When we feel like we want to play safe, we should try to change the strategy but not the attitude. Let's be careful. Let's take fewer risks, but let's stay focused on getting it right.
This is quite common when we introduce a new effect in our shows. Our feelings will be different and unique, so it is quite normal to have this kind of play-safe attitude. Gradually, we will gain confidence, and we will be letting ourselves go a little more. Let's be patient. We can never win these battles in a day. Over time, the feeling of wanting to play safe will disappear, and we will only concentrate on enjoying our wonderful job.

The Adrenaline

Our body produces adrenaline when we are in front of situations that carry some risk. Also, our brains tell our bodies to be in tension. The interpretation of these situations is subjective, and thus, the amount of stress we experience depends on each one of us.

Our body can suffer such high muscle tension that will keep us shrunken and sore. We could also experience a mental and muscle block that prevents us from letting go. If this happens, we will be lost. We will not know how to live up to the circumstances, reflected in an unbearable sense of anxiety and burden.

On the other hand, having a certain amount of adrenaline in our body can be beneficial. If we try to keep a challenging attitude towards risky situations, we will visualize them as challenges we can overcome. The right amount of muscle tension and well-channelled nerves will play in our favour and keep us alert.

Our nervous system is a difficult thing to control consciously. Specific meditation exercises based on our breathing can help us manage our nerves while at the same time, we could also increase the level of self-awareness. Once again, we can find help in psychologists. These professionals will know better, and they can recommend the different techniques that exist to control our nervous system.

The more you know about yourself, the easier will be to get ready to overcome the unexpected.

Final Thoughts

When we force a mistake, we must be able to get out of it. It may seem trivial but let me say it. If we are not prepared enough to get out of difficult situations, we should never create them artificially. That would be very stupid of us, wouldn't it?

We must always keep in mind that forcing a trouble situation could increase the climax of an effect, but this will only happen if we get out of it and "in one piece".

As Master Colombini would say: if you try to fail and you succeed, which of the two things will you have achieved? My advice is not to complicate your life unnecessarily if you do not know how you will manage beforehand.

Please, always remember the most important tip: if you fail, do not feel guilty. Take note of what happened, and work towards never getting back to the point of no return.

6. Creativity

"Never imagine yourself not to be otherwise than what it might appear to others that what you were or might have been was not otherwise than what you had been would have appeared to them to be otherwise." – Alice in Wonderland (Lewis Carroll)

All the magicians attending the 2010 national congress in La Coruña crowded the Rosalía de Castro theatre. That evening, we were all looking forward to enjoying the long-awaited gala titled "The greatest creative magicians". The cast included many kinds of international performers, all of them rated as top world-class illusionists.

As the curtain opened for the show to begin, they presented the audience a lonely large movie screen on stage. After a few moments of uncertainty sinking in, the image of Mago Anton materialized on the screen. He gave everyone a warm welcome and set out to explain what creativity was: *"Creativity is...."* (he was silent not knowing what else to say), *"creativity is... hum...what the heck is creativity?"*

The Mystery of Creativity

One of the magic world features is the existence of many small and significant secrets that make magic an exceptional discipline. Despite being able to master great manipulative techniques, excellent psychological skills for audience management, and an unlimited passion for building outstanding magical presentations, creativity is something that all magicians talk about, but whose mastery is never understood.

For decades, scientists have tried to study creativity and answer all the "whys" related to it. Just as scientists measure intelligence with IQ (Intelligence Quotient); they have made attempts to create tests to quantify creativity. The result to date has been a total failure.

I must admit I did not include any specific chapter on creativity in this project's initial sketch. However, as I have been writing a lot about the rehearsal of the mistakes, at this point, I resist to abandon you by saying that from here, only the creativity of each artist will take him further. I do not think it would be fair. At least, I would like to share my research and reflections on this untamed muse. I do not want to dogmatize anything, since already many people have written about it before. Please, allow me just to give my complementary vision. It will fill me with great happiness knowing that I may help a reader get closer to finding her (the muse) and that when you finally meet her, you will recognize her.

We must understand from the beginning that we will not marry creativity and settle in with her in our forest house. The creative muse will only come if we have a restless attitude, and she will stay for some time, as long as we take care of her and treat her well. She will be free to leave and return after a while, but it will not be only up to us.

Why Creativity?

Art is mistakenly associated with creativity. Many people even mix the meaning of "artistic expression" and "creative expression". At this point, I think there is no need to convince anyone that what some people may find sublime art; others may find it monotonous and boring. In the same way, creativity can manifest itself in many other aspects of life.

Focusing on our discipline, creativity in magic is very well valued, and the creative artist always leaves a unique mark. That is one of the reasons why magic stands within the performing arts. And it is an art because it excites the spectator who enjoys it.

Nowadays, magic is unfortunately still considered a minor art, although most magicians find it hard to admit it. We should not be so surprised, since only recently, in the nineteenth century, magic made the leap to the stage thanks to the French magician, Robert Houdin. The audience enjoys our shows and finds them fascinating, but perhaps, they still consider magic as a cool skill, such as juggling knives or taming animals.

Magicians have an innate hunger for creating original acts and effects. I think that it can only be a good sign. This looks like **the path that every major art under development seems to follow.** Dance is an excellent example of it. Until the early twentieth century, dance was not considered a serious performing art. Thanks to Isadora Duncan's work, choreographies began to be loaded with high emotional content, which had never been done before. Between 1926 and 1935, dance experienced a turning point in public opinion. Audiences started to consider dancers for their tremendous efforts to perform with maximum perfection sequences of human movement. They finally amazed even the most ignorant spectators.

Wouldn't it be wonderful if people admired magicians on that same level of artists? For now, only a few magicians make it.

Who is Creative?

By definition, humans are intelligent beings, but we do not necessarily have to develop as creative people. It is a potential that we all have to a greater or lesser extent and that we can all cultivate.

Some people believe that one can only be born creative. I am not going to deny that there have been great geniuses with tremendous innate creative potential. However, history shows us that a passion for work and a constant effort to evolve lead to awakening creativity and inviting it to stay with us, at least for a while.

In parallel with his fascinating theory of multiple intelligences, researcher and psychologist Howard Gardner argues that creative potential only has the possibility of awakening during the development of specific activities. The beauty of these varies with each person. Like all studies on creativity, it is not scientific dogma, but it is a theory that I love.

It is no coincidence that parents put an instrument in their children's hands or sign them up to painting classes. These activities are designed to awaken the creative potential. However, if the little boy stays playing in his room, he could also awaken creativity in a different way, by transforming the world around him to his taste when he plays. Children can do that without anyone imposing them rules. They create their particular world with their logic, and they even add some details that are full of emotions. These can be so powerful that even in adulthood, we will remember them perfectly when we yearn for the distant days of childhood play.

Early recognition of a particular creative expression can come to discover a future virtuoso musician, painter... and even magician!

Although it can be very comfortable for parents, it is never a bad idea to remind us that consuming television programs does not enhance creativity. On the contrary, it atrophies our brains.

The boy Wolfgang Amadeus did not spend his childhood in front of the silly box. However, he is a clear example of an early creative prodigy that faded away. The early comfort and fame achieved by this genius led Mozart to abandon his immense creative potential at an unusually early age.

An example of the opposite would be Martha Graham, the big creative star who successfully took dance to the top. This dancer, who even founded her own company, was inexhaustibly enterprising and adversity could not beat her. If any of her projects failed, she learned her lesson well, and within time she always returned to the fighting pit with even more energy.

Howard Gardner defines the creative individual as the person who solves problems regularly and dares to create new solutions. His creations, which may prove novel at first, eventually end up being accepted in a specific cultural context.

Creative Artists Traits

It is the complex system of human qualities such as expertise, intelligence, talent, and restlessness, which establishes each person's creative potential. Most of them are not quantifiable, which is why their product, creativity, is challenging to quantify or even explain. Effort and work provide tickets to win the grand prize. Luck can turn up too, but you are more likely to run into creativity when looking for her.

It is exceptionally complicated, close to impossible, to be creative in a discipline that is not well known. After all, to create is to associate existing concepts but in a new way. That is the idea that we will eventually put into practice. First, we must all achieve absolute dominance of the field in question to be able to create something new. The innate is not creativity, but the restlessness and curiosity we show from the very first moments of the learning period. This concern leads us to question the basic principles of any discipline and learn the existing laws. **Curiosity leads us to the limits of what is already explored, and self-confidence is the one that pushes us to go further beyond.**

I invite you to reflect on a statement from I.I. Rabi: "*I think scientists are the Peter Pans of humanity. They never grow up, and they keep their curiosity. Once you are sophisticated, you know too much, far too much.*"

Einstein was always proud of his unique imaginative skills: "*When I examine myself and my thinking methods, I conclude that the gift of fantasy has meant more to me than my talent for absorbing true knowledge*".

However, although any person with appropriate qualities could show a notable "creative potential", it could be not enough to succeed. Some external factors will have great relevance in the creative process.

External Factors

All creatives have three kinds of relationships that influence their project: the relationship with the first knowledge, the relationship with oneself, and the relationship with the outside world.

a) Relationship with the first knowledge

Before presenting any new challenge in a field, it is necessary to understand it deeply.

Sometimes, we hear magicians say they had invented a gimmick or a technique, when in fact they had already been developed. It proves two important things: we can also achieve knowledge through personal development, and it is advisable to know quite well how things work before wanting to change them.

A good teacher is one who prepares the student to go further than the master has ever gone. In opposition to the Spanish education system, I think that students should be prepared not only by giving them a master class but also by pushing them to achieve knowledge through synthesis and developing their own work.

If this learning process is followed right, it will be easier for the students to have the opportunity to generate some concern that may lead them to question the most basic principles. When the moment comes, the students will be prepared with a great knowledge collection that could take them to explore new unsuspected limits.

b) Relationship with oneself

It is almost impossible to be creative if there is no passionate interest in the work we develop ourselves. We process the learned lessons in our own way, and from there, we may reach the possibility to develop what we are really interested in.

We all have great plans and great ideas, but have you ever wondered why only some magicians start working on them? The odd thing is that only a few of them come to an end... The secret, in most cases, has to do with commitment.

Commitment in each person reveals in different situations. For a boxer is to get up from the canvas, for cyclists is to continue climbing the mountain when they are no longer strong, for athletes is to finish the race even if they know that they will no longer win...

Michael Jordan once mentioned in an interview: "*Heart is what separates the good from the great*". This great basketball player referred in those words to the origin of all commitment.

The genuinely committed creative magician is the one that takes his plan into action and who persists in his work without abandoning when encountering the first obstacles. You do not know how far you will go, but you can be sure that you will be working hard to complete your journey.

Our interest in the cause and our trust in ourselves (self-confidence) helps us resist failures, even if they come one after the other. It is the invisible force that makes us move forward despite not receiving any compensation.

If we want to get to some worthwhile place, as creative people, we have no choice. We must commit to ourselves and our work.

c) Relationship with the outside world

From the world, we learn, and for the world we create. We continually feed our activities and work back to the world around us. It is something we cannot help.

Positive feedback strengthens our confidence. It is a crucial factor that enhances or diminishes our interest in developing a project, and it encourages our curiosity towards the unknown.

Different types of relationships with other people can encourage our work. I think we can go much further with companionship relationships and mutual support than rivalry with our colleagues.

I want to point out that a small dose of rivalry is supposed to be healthy for every artist. However, it does not make sense to strive on putting obstacles on each other all the time. Nobody deserves to be continuously discredited for one's work.

It is also worth mentioning that encouragement and criticisms offered by people close to us could always add up to the cause and help us complete our creations.

For sure, we will encounter reviews which we must learn how to filter and to process wisely. Constructively taking criticism can mean discovering a new perspective, and that could mean the final push towards the perfection of our work.

Throughout history, there have been many times when the creations of some composers, some painters or some sculptors, never had the proper feedback while the creator was still alive. It is due to a lack of synchronism between the social imaginary and the creator's work. The evolution of the social imaginary leads them to meet over the years. Luckily, in the magic world, this does not happen very often.

We cannot prevent the outside world from taking an influence on us. From the world, we obtain our knowledge, and to the world, we pour our work.

The Marginality of the Creative Artist

Nowadays, we live in a world full of comforts, but also full of noise and distractions. Sometimes we should take a break, meditate, do self-assessments and dream about the future.

Great creative characters throughout history have been considered eccentric hermits who lived far from society. The truth is that they sought to move away from the comforts of the world to awaken their creativity in limit situations.

Do not make the mistake of thinking that a creative person should live isolated from the world. The creative knows the world well. Perhaps this "isolation" only happens during a particular phase of the synthesis of his creativity, when he takes a step back and moves away from distractions to create something. His creation will be returned to the world eventually and thus, with this gesture, the creative will purchase his ticket back from his chosen marginality.

The world around the creative one influences him as a human being and over his personal development. We could also understand the chosen marginality as an effort to find a general perspective or even discover a completely new point of view.

In our daily work, society pushes us to follow specific schedules, fulfil a million responsibilities, or worry about things that we do not care about in the end. Are we not great masters of making up excuses to deceive ourselves? In order to be creative, we need to invest time and effort into our work. Taking a break from the world will leave us in the perfect situation: only us and our work to worry about.

We can only understand certain concepts from a marginal position. A sample of that is happening while I am writing these lines. This book is a personal project that I have finally managed to start, but at thousands of miles from my home!

The marginality of the creative one should not be permanent. The world keeps spinning even if we get off for a while. We must keep an eye on it as things evolve, on others' creations and on the possible new ideas that are emerging.

Where is Creativity?

We should not worry about defining creativity since it is a subjective concept to each person and the world around us. What magicians want to know is where to find creativity. This quest can become an obsession. My advice is to enjoy the exploration because it is a beautiful enriching process.

Before we go on this quest, we must not pressure on ourselves. Do not confuse this with the motivation to be creative, which is a major element for success. According to Teresa Amabile, if we are lucky enough to enjoy a total absence of external pressures (usually fear of being judged by others), the creative solution will be presented more accessible. That said, there is no guarantee of success. Our set of qualities, innate and cultivated ones, will play an important role. These will help us move on and get up every time we fail or go through long periods without compensation.

In this expedition, the treasure map will be drawn little by little, as we make progress through the different stages:

-   Initial Training

Once we have an initial interest in a discipline or a field, we begin a knowledge acquisition and skill development period.

Have you ever stopped to think about how music stars are born? All singers learn by singing others' songs by modulating their voice and trying to be faithful to the original piece. Eventually, they will know themselves better, and they will apply small changes to those compositions in the search for their own style. The magicians follow the same process. We start by learning published effects and by copying the presentations of the great masters. Then, we will slowly be transforming ourselves into something else, a new artist with a first and a last name.

Only the great creative magicians strive on innovation from the early stages, at least with their presentations of the effects. It is not enough to mimic the presentations they learn from the books, but they try to give their personal touch to the routines.

Magic is a discipline that in most cases, is learned in a self-taught way, by reading books and by using the imagination. Suppose the magician's apprentice reveals a constant fondness for dismembering and readapting other magicians' effects. In that case, he will not drive his master crazy as usually happens with the musicians' first creative attempts. This initial experimentation will prove crucial in the development of the creations of the future illusionist.

This first training phase should be full of events that get a deep impression on us. Our goal must be to soak ourselves with knowledge as if we were sponges. And in case our memory cannot remember everything, we should always keep a small notebook at hand where we can write facts, thoughts, and ideas. Do not let anything slip away!

- **Mastery**

At the end of the learning period, we will achieve mastery. In other words, that means a superb knowledge of the field. According to the findings of Howard Gardner's studies, it seems that at least ten years of continuous work are required to achieve such mastery. This is a must to be able to take an important creative twist.

The creative master is aware of the new developments, but he does not stop to procrastinate, and he is willing to leave his safe zone and face new challenges. It is the confidence gained after years of work what pushes the master towards such audacity.

Staying receptive to other people's new findings will always be beneficial. It can bring fundamental knowledge to our work and ward off the possibility of reinventing something that was already there.

- **Marginality**

During this phase of exploration, the creative one can benefit from a temporary retirement from the world. We must take this marginality with enthusiasm, and we should always bear in mind the goal we pursue.

Picasso described the moments when he was aware of the risks he assumed: "*Painting is freedom. If you take a leap, you may fall on the wrong side of the rope. But if you are not willing to take the risk of*

114

breaking your neck, what's the use? You'd better not take the leap anyway".

The learning phase up to mastery should be full of events that will make us come across some unexpected discoveries with some luck. In the quiet periods, we will evoke past experiences, we will remember those specific ideas that we once had, and we will process them.

The monotony of a quiet life stimulates our minds. If the creative one needs to stay away from the world for a while, it is only to seek this much-needed stimulus.

- **Criticism and Compliments**

The last phase of the creative process is the return of the work results to the world.

When we finally show our creation to others, we are hoping to draw some attention. We may have higher or lower expectations regarding the acceptance of our work. As long as our colleagues in the field consider the novelty worthy of attention, we will have already succeeded as creative artists.

This phase is vital because it means the completion of our work to some extent. Our work could be modified or reinvented in the long term, although it will always bear the label of its first premiere.

It is not uncommon to see some magicians' acts evolving over time. I am sure this happens with most of them. It may be about some subtle details, or sometimes even significant changes are revealed, but the audience will always recall the emotions felt the night they saw those acts for the first time.

We need to be smart when digesting the reviews and we should learn how to filter both the good ones and the bad ones. We must constructively take on the negative reviews, while the positive ones need to help us strengthen our confidence in our work.

Filtering is necessary, as some people's envy and wickedness direct their comments' intention and subjectivity. On the other hand, it is not healthy to believe all positive reviews since they could come from flatterers without objectivity or from people who simply do not want to cause us trouble.

Our real friends are the ones who use a carrot-and-stick policy, as appropriate. They are not allowing us to fall into depression when they encourage us to get up after a fall, and they are bringing it to our attention when our ego swells up too much. Treat your friends like they are gold because they are a great treasure of yours.

Great creatives are only magicians whose acts or techniques will become so appreciated that they will set a turning point in some discipline or speciality in magic. The magicians coming after them will study these great artists, and their creations will inspire them.

Why shouldn't you, my friend, be the next great creative magician?

How Long Does Creativity last?

Like so many other things in life, creativity does not last forever. Perhaps, only diamonds do. It is the ordinary course of life. Comfort overcomes curiosity, and we get to the point where we abandon the pursuit of the creative muse.

It seems even cruel to say it after so much effort and work. When we finally start a relationship with creativity, she never intends to stay with us forever.

Our crush's duration with creativity is variable, and it always seems to be shorter than desired. It always depends on ourselves and the same external factors that led us to find her.

Success brings us to comfort, and it causes creativity to fade quickly. I am not saying we do not deserve some comfort from time to time, but we need to understand that we cannot have both at the same time.

If you look at the great creatives and what they often call their "great innovative creations", those almost always take place after ten years of work. Only a few of them come to conclude a second masterpiece which, if ever produced, it is only at the end of another long period of minor creations.

How can I be Creative?

Perhaps, dear reader, you are worried about not considering yourself a person of divergent thinking. Do you think you are not intelligent enough and do not possess any of the necessary qualities described in this chapter to create something on your own? Let me tell you one thing: you are mistaken.

For starters, if you have come all this way, you have already shown an initial interest in creating something innovative. It can be a technique, a presentation or even an act. The seed is already there. You just need to learn how to water it and maybe this section could give you some ideas.

Do not put limits on yourself, but small goals. Always keep on learning and try to become an expert about those things that you find interesting.

Open your eyes and experiment during your training process. Do not gobble up information without processing it well. Try to understand the reasons. Do not hinder your curiosity, investigate and ask around everything you need.

Be patient in achieving the farthest goals. Do not worry about the obstacles that may appear in the future. Do not obsess about getting there fast in the last phase. Enjoy every stage of the process. Focus on getting better, rather than being good.

Surround yourself with good friends to seek support. That does not mean you do not believe in your own ideas, but it helps you keep an open mind. Believe in yourself and live the present.

Be inspired by your work and your project. Try to maintain a steady and continuous work pace. As Freud would say, "*if inspiration does not come to you, do not hesitate to meet her halfway*". Have guts. Take a leap. And if you fall, get up!

Do not just isolate yourself in the discipline you love and start showing some interest in others' projects. Maybe, you could learn from each other.

Stay away from your magic props from time to time and do things that have nothing to do with magic. Before a magician, you are a person, and you need to have a life outside of magic. It will help you have a more interesting personality and better connect with your audience when it comes to performing. Besides, life has an endless list of wonderful things to enjoy.

Buy two or three notebooks, and always have one handy, even under the pillow. Write down the ideas, reflections, and thoughts you have in your everyday life. Occasionally, go through the pages and enjoy remembering the things you have been writing down.

Learn from your failures. Be aware that you can only know whether you are following the right path by the old method of trial and error. If you stop to think about it, one might say that the great creative ones achieved their goals almost by increasing the likelihood, since they came to produce many more creations than the rest of magicians. That collection includes the good creations and the not so good ones.

Prodigy is overrated. It is not a standard quality with the same quantity in all great creators. Focus on your virtues and set your flaws aside. Be aware of the existence of both.

When you have a plan or idea, sit down and calmly plan the route you want to follow. It will help you know at any given time how far you need to go and the progress you are making. If you do not take care of your own motivation, no one else may do it for you.

Be optimistic and realistic at the same time with the degree of commitment you want to have and of course, do not underestimate how difficult it can be to get what you have set out to do.

And if you have doubts, look for the answer in your heart...

"I claim to be an average man of less than average ability. I admit I am not intellectually brilliant. But I do not care. There is a limit to the development of the intellect, but none for the heart."

– Mahatma Gandhi

...

..

.

From the start of my investigations, I have found many books in the market that talk about creativity. Still, very few include a method that I have liked with practical exercises to develop it. Here is my favourite one.

If you are interested in developing your creativity, I recommend the book *"The Secret of the Highly Creative Thinker"*, by Dorte Nielsen and Sarah Thurber. I discovered this book by chance on a visit to the Sydney Museum of Modern Art shop. On its pages, the authors describe different exercises that you can do for twenty-one days to develop your ability to establish connections and, consequently, your creativity. You will have a lot of fun while doing those exercises, and you will improve some specific capabilities. It is a gem. And if you like the method, you will find additional activities in the book *"Creative Thinker's Exercise book"* by the same authors.

7. Final Thoughts

"The time always comes when we discover that we knew much more than we thought we did." – Seeing (José Saramago)

Throughout this book's chapters, I have guided you through the different aspects of the mistakes on stage. We have also seen how to play with failure. Many people judge books by their cover or by the number of pages they have. Personally, the value I give a book is related to how much it makes me think. I invite you to set the value of *Rehearsing Your Mistakes* that way.

I hope you never find yourself afraid of failure, nor do you consider it your enemy. Just like with the ocean, you must be respectful and know how to enjoy it properly.

The mistake is a friend that will turn up without any warning, and at the time you expect the least. Your preparation as an artist should train you to have the skills to give it a warm welcome in your show, and with the biggest smile on your face.

No one escapes the possibility of receiving this unexpected visit sooner or later. Do not be caught in a mere statement of good resolutions and work on improving your improvisation skills. Remember, improv is a secret weapon that can save your life in all performing arts.

Keep your eyes open and stay receptive to everything around you. Magic is your game, and the stage is your playroom; therefore, you set the rules. Has anyone not ever said to you: "This is my house and here we play by my rules..."?

Be the first one to believe in what you do. It is the first step to convey the right emotions to the audience. Trust your skills and try to enjoy even the worst moments.

Give your rehearsal plenty of time. Not knowing or not analysing the possible random variables surrounding your show leaves success in the hands of chance. You have heard it a thousand times in your life: prevention is better than cure.

Mastering a magic act or an entire show also involves knowing its weaknesses well and being aware of the script's possible deviations and the risk they could bring along.

Learn from your experiences, from your rehearsals and from anything you see around you. Keep a positive attitude towards the risks you locate and cultivate your imagination so you can enjoy finding ways out and rescue plans.

You are not alone. Hey! Still not talking about aliens! Other colleague magicians may have encountered similar situations. Sharing and discussing points of view will lead you to better results, and way faster than always working on your own.

Get used to using questions that start with "what if...?". Imagination has no limits, dare to explore. There are still many wonders to be discovered out there!

Try to find out where you have the most potential to develop creativity. Research, learn and experiment. The commitment to your work will "make the planets align" sooner or later, and your reward will come.

The creative process has a time, a specific space and an inner world in every magician. It is a path of personal growth, research, imaginative experimentation, and development of critical thinking. In the end, you will find magic as a true art capable of thrilling people and of bringing light into their lives.

Are you in for making mistakes?

Undoubtedly, your show has a good repertoire of effects which even if they are not original, you will gradually season with small personal details.

The small details have a bit of a "butterfly effect", although they are **simple subtleties, they can make big differences in presentations of the same effect.**

Here are some examples of classic and commercial effects that would not be the same without the flaws. We will also see some effects that are enhanced by the forced artificial mistakes. Maybe, they will even inspire you to give a little twist to some of your routines.

Cards on a sword

Many magicians perform this effect, and almost all of them in the same way. When throwing the cards into the air, the artist shows his skills with the weapon and the three chosen cards appear along the blade. One of them appears in the tip, another near the base and the last one in the middle of the sword.

Years ago, while reflecting on this effect with Jesus Duque, we concluded that this classic production of the cards had a weak moment because of the inconsistency of the position where the pinned cards appeared.

That conversation led me to think about making a little variation. I asked myself what would happen if someone really had those skills to pin cards in the air with a sword: with the cards being so light, it would be impossible to pin them very deep in the blade of the sword. It would probably only be possible to pin them with the tip of the sword.

I applied the changes and presented the effect at a gala where I worked with other colleagues. That night, I noticed a massive difference in the reactions I got from my skills with the sword. Total silence from the audience!

Well, that happened only for a few moments... Let me finish the story. I meant that no one cheered me up for having pinned the cards with the sword. From the stalls, the audience could see nothing but a single card on the tip of the blade. A moment of real suspense was created after a few seconds when I started to separate the cards with my hand and displaced them along the sword's blade. That made the audience ovation louder than ever, and I even had not revealed that those were indeed the chosen cards yet!

No words needed and with only minimal body language (no more than a raised eyebrow), the audience had convinced themselves of my failure.

Since then, I always perform this effect in the same way.

It is a small detail that suppresses an incongruity. It creates a short moment of suspense for a reasonable possible failure, and it enhances a spontaneous ovation from the audience.

Guessing a card

Who has not ever done any guessing effect on a card? Possibly, the first effect you learned was about guessing a card from a spectator in one way or another.

There is a vast collection of routines whose primary effect is nothing more than taking a guess on a card under impossible conditions for the magician. I often think that magicians are too fortunate that every possible variant of the ending is interpreted by the lay audience as a different routine, even if the effect is the same.

In some routines, the card is freely chosen by the spectator, while in others, it is a forced card. Either way, once the magician knows the chosen card, it is just a matter of deciding the preferred way to reveal it.

If we incorporate an artificial mistake in our guessing, later we can reach a higher climax in the finale.

For example, some magicians pick to reveal the chosen card in a drawing while reading the spectator's mind. Martin Lewis had the idea of making this effect fail to create a more robust and better finale. Surely, at some point, Martin had probably failed the revelation with a drawing or perhaps, he had wondered how he would solve such a situation if it were to happen to him. I do not know what it was before, the egg or the chicken. If I ever get the chance, I will ask Mr Lewis.

Just in case you do not know the effect, let me describe it here: After drawing a card on a pad and failing the spectator's choice, Martin Lewis explains, as a gag, that what he had drawn was nothing different than the first card of a full deck. A witty excuse that rips off some grins from the audience, but it still leaves the spectators in a state of disappointment.

But the routine does not end there. Martin then adds a couple of perspective details to the drawing to insist on his excuse. It is when the audience starts to feel that the magician is trying to regain his status back. And this may also help him get the audience on the artist's side by breaking the tension a little, while Martin takes control of the situation (as if saying "keep calm, it is all under control").

The grand finale is a very powerful magic effect, in which the chosen card magically rises from the deck of cards in the drawing. In addition to the magician guessing the card, we now have a visual magic effect with an animated picture. Of course, people are amazed, and they always give a passionate ovation at this wonder. The magician has amended his mistake completely. And as if it were not enough, the assistant takes home the signed drawing that will be a great memory of the experience forever.

Many commercial effects work in the same way. These routines consist of guessing a card but with an artificial failure and a proper rescue plan as a finale, which helps to get a more significant impact. The price you pay for such a routine in a magic shop is not only related to the cost of the material, but also to the idea that allows you to improve a divination act.

Masuda's Wow presents itself as an effect to be performed with an artificial failure. In this routine, the spectator signs a card which is then lost in the deck. After some magic moves, the magician selects a card and places it into a small metal grid. When the spectators look at this card through the grid, they immediately think the magician has failed. Right after that moment of disappointment, the magical effect suddenly happens when the card in the grid is transformed into the chosen signed card in a very visual way.

I could write thousands of pages about classic and commercial routines that enhance the divination of a card. But remember that my goal here is to make you think. These two examples I just mentioned should be enough to prove my point. The Cardiographic and the Wow are very popular routines because they have a big impact on the audience. But there are many more out there. If you have some time, you can create a list of commercial effects that you know that benefit from some artificial mistakes.

The Invisible Deck

In Spain, it is not common for people to know the poker cards, although the social imaginary conceives that magicians use them. As a result, we often come across situations on stage when spectators name the wrong suites, or even some of them directly ask the magician for the Spanish deck.

In the classic presentation of the "invisible deck", the assistant picks a card from an imaginary deck. In Spain, if the magician does not specify that it is an imaginary set of poker cards, there is a high risk of having the assistant going for the golds, the swords, the cups or the clubs.

Bodie Blake, a magician from Argentina, had the idea of improving this effect by playing with the two possible situations that could happen when the assistant imagines "picking a card": with the card belonging to the French deck or the Spanish deck. In this new version of the invisible deck, whatever happens when the assistant names the chosen card, the magician looks surprised and hesitantly continues with the performance. The magician's body language soon reveals that something is not going well, although the audience still does not identify what it could be.

When the deck finally appears, the audience notices that all the cards belong to a different deck from the one that the assistant picked his. He could not have known that! The magician is in big trouble now! If the assistant chose a card from the French deck, the deck produced by the magician in his hands is a Spanish deck. And if the card selected by the assistant belonged to the Spanish deck, the deck produced by the magician is the French one.

The great climax is reached when, despite the confusion with the decks, a face-down card is found, and that is none other than the card chosen by the spectator, despite belonging to a different deck! A mind-blowing magic effect.

The classic effect of the invisible deck already had an extraordinarily strong impact on spectators. As we just observed, that impact can be even more significant if the audience understands that the magician has committed a slip and that impossibility conditions are even more remarkable. Can you imagine the reaction of that spectator who has already seen another magician performing the classic version of the invisible deck... isn't this new version pure magic?

If you want to learn more about this effect, you will find it with the name "Supermental Deck" on the pages of the book *Automatically Yours,* first published in 1989 by Bodie Blake. I know that there are similar versions on the market by other magicians, although my research indicates that they released those later.

Telepathy

Most of the times, this routine is performed by a couple of artists. Telepathy happens when one of them, usually blindfolded, is guessing the objects shown, either by the audience or by own companion. Anything the audience can produce is valid: watches, keys, phones, etc.

The impact of this classic of mentalism is remarkably high. For several minutes, the audience stays in shock while the artist wearing the blindfold is naming all the objects, one after the other, even with small details such as the colour, the brand, etc.

But one of the aspects of mentalism is that it must look authentic for it to work. To convey this feat's great difficulty, artists in this routine never get one hundred per cent of the objects right. They take the liberty of making small mistakes from time to time. These are flaws that fall into the script.

In this fantastic routine, the artificial mistakes make the artists more human, make them closer to the audience, and put everyone on the same side.

Bill Transposition

Many magicians have a transposition or travel effect of a borrowed bill in their repertoire. The basic idea is that the note vanishes from one place, to later appear in an impossible location, such as inside a lemon or an orange.

The disappearance of the bill is an effect that can be performed in many ways. A false deposit or a devil's handkerchief would perfectly fulfil the mission of making it evaporate, and this would get the first ovation from the audience without any doubt.

However, many artists choose to increase the impact of this effect by simulating a mistake: the bill gets completely destroyed in an "involuntary" way (for example, with fire). Of course, the error does not get any ovation from the audience, but silence. Some magicians take the opportunity to create a dramatic atmosphere, others to create a comic situation. As we have seen in chapter 4, each magician picks his use of the artificial mistake based on his character on stage.

When the bill finally reappears, the climax is very intense. In addition to the bill's impossible transposition, the total restoration of the destroyed note is added to the magical effect.

All versions of impossible transposition effects with things borrowed by spectators will gain magic power if we add an artificial mistake that looks like it wrecks the item. The spectators will go home twice as happy, for having enjoyed the show and for having recovered their object in perfect conditions.

My friend Hector Sansegundo on his street show presents the effect of an impossible ring transposition with a brilliant presentation based on a mistake. Although Hector has not made available yet to the world the rights to perform this routine, he allowed me to describe it on this book.

> ➢ **Upwards** *(a transposition effect from Hector Sansegundo)*

The conditions in which Hector presents this effect are those known by every artist who performs in the street: with the possibility of having wind, with the prospect of being surrounded by the audience, with the possibility of working without a curtain, without any stage, without a roof, etc.

Upwards consists of two phases. The first one is a skill contest: Hector claims that he can explode a helium balloon (held by a child) with a pin and a slingshot!! This routine is quite comical itself, and Hector takes advantage of it with many gags that make the audience laugh a lot. Once Hector proves that he can blow up the helium balloon with a slingshot and a pin, the audience gives the magician a nice ovation for his skills. Of course, at no time is the child in danger here.

The second phase of *Upwards* begins when Hector decides to introduce in the demonstration a personal object from someone in the audience, someone's finger-ring. This ring is inserted into a small cloth bag, which the owner of the ring then proceeds to tie to another pair of helium balloons held by the child who was already on stage.

Then, Hector states that he will try to repeat his feat, but now he asks the child to release the balloons into the air at the count of three, to attempt to make them explode while they are on the air. Suddenly, the situation has become more interesting for the audience: the ring is tied to the balloons that are pulling upwards hard, and only the child's hand keeps them under control. The audience's tension and interest get increased even more when Hector puts on a blindfold to make things even a little more complicated. At this point, the tension and expectations are top-high. The audience has already seen that the artist could blow up a balloon just by shooting a pin, but will he now be able to pop two balloons in the air and with his eyes behind a blindfold? Everyone is aware of the risky destination of the spectator's ring if something goes wrong.

Thanks to the magician's speech and a very well measured rhythm *(timing)*, the child ends up releasing the balloons early, when Hector has not even come to put the pin in the slingshot yet. The balloons quickly rise into the sky, taking the spectator's ring with them. Goodbye, ring!! This highly visual moment generates a gigantic dramatic atmosphere, mixed with nervous laughter, feelings of wonder, faces of fascination and some other killer looks. Everyone knows that by now, it is already impossible to get the balloons down. They are already hundreds of meters away above their heads. The assistant spectator has lost her ring forever! The mistake seems accidental, but the most important thing is that Hector reinforces that fact with his attitude. He holds up long enough for the assistant, the child and the rest of the audience to believe that what has happened was totally unexpected.

Eventually, Hector regains control of the situation with jokes that break the tension, although part of the audience may still think that the magician needs a miracle to get out of such a big trouble.

He achieves an impossible finale when the ring reappears inside a pen in the hands of the ring owner who, in a mixture of disbelief and joy, breathes relieved for having got her precious object back.

The audience reactions are incredible when they see that everything had been scripted within the show. They come to realize then that they had seen a great hoax. If we add to this hoax the impossibility of the magic effect, we get a very strong climax.

Without a doubt, after enjoying *Upwards,* the spectators go home with a good story to tell. They have lived some memorable moments!

...

..

.

And these are just a few use cases of artificial mistakes that have their application in the real world. If you take a few moments to reflect, several more effects which make use of artificial mistakes may come to your mind.

For now, it is time for us to say goodbye here.

I really hope that you enjoyed this book. I wrote it from my heart. If it made you think, even if it was just a little bit, I will be happy.

And if I made any mistakes along these pages, let me take note of them, and I promise I will improve it in future editions.

Feel free to send me your feedback to magia@angelsimal.com

Warm Regards!

Acknowledgements

It has been about two years since I decided to set sails on the greatest adventure of my life. I left Spain for good and started a new life, literally on the other side of the world: New Zealand.

I needed a break that I could only reach by disconnecting completely. I knew it would not be easy, but I was genuinely excited about discovering a new world and starting from scratch only with the help of my skills and knowledge.

A couple of weeks before leaving, I was struck by a sign they had on the wall in a restaurant in Suances: "*Anyone who knows the art of living with oneself will ignore boredom*". During this retreat, I have understood the wisdom of those words. When you go from a hectic life to a laid-back one, the days seem longer, and it gives you a lot of time to think and reflect. The consequence is that you gradually get to know yourself better.

From the moment I arrived in this fascinating country, I started to try new things, and to invest that much free time in project ideas that I had had on my imaginary shelves for a long time. *Rehearsing Your Mistakes* was one of them.

Writing this book has taken me almost two years of work. The idea and my personal experience came from Spain, but I have also needed to read a great variety of books, I have made a lot of research, and I even got in touch with different experts. It has been so exciting!

This is my first book, and at the moment, I have no idea if there will be more in the future. Finishing a project like this is pretty rewarding for me, and that is why I would like to share with you the following acknowledgements:

A big thanks…

To my friend Mayte Gamo, great professional of psychology, who supported me from the very beginning with this project and guided me on the right direction in my research on creativity and psychological aspects of people's failures.

To Quique Álvarez, president of the Valladolid Magic Club for many years, because the seed for his book's idea would not have been planted in me without his mini-lecture "*Magic Theory and How to Rehearse*".

To Howard Gardner, for sharing with all humankind his magnificent theory of multiple intelligences. His research on creativity deserves, without any doubt, to be widely spread among the different education systems.

To Norbert Ferré, for writing the best foreword for this project.

To Ken Follet, because without the publication of his method for writing a book, I would not have known how to start sorting my ideas.

To the Wellington Magic Club, for giving me such a nice place to hang out. Thanks for sharing awesome magic evenings during my long stay in this wonderful country.

To my family, especially to my mother, for her unconditional support and for always being there in the good and the bad times. You are the best.

To Rene Becker, the improv teacher who taught me all the useful techniques and the nice secrets of improvisation theatre.

To my friends from Palencia, professional critic folks of my work, who always pointed me in the right direction.

To all the members of the Valladolid Magic Club, for their friendship.

To my grandfather Julio, the first one who thought that my magic was worth to be performed in front of an audience. Thanks for convincing me to perform at the Germany Pals Club.

To my brothers, for their help and their comments every time I try a new effect. I do not know what I would do without you.

To Juan Carlos Valerón, for the great nights of magical football that he performed for so many years.

To Jesus Duque, for sharing with me his way of understanding magic and for making me think.

To Fernando Arribas, for opening the gates of the magic world to me for the first time.

To Luisan, Tuco and Sonia, Amadeo and Blanca, Dany, Lucia, Jose, Nano, Hector and Marta, Eric and Juanky, for so many laughs and magical days we have spent together.

To my American friends, for all those great summers when we were teenagers. I had the time of my life with you.

To my New Zealand friends, for taking care of me and making me feel at home.

To the Council of Palencia, for trusting me with the organization of the Magic Castle festival.

To all those who ever closed a door in front of me, because without them I may not have come to try harder and perhaps I would not be here now.

To all those who have trusted me with my work in magic, because I absolutely enjoyed every moment of all those performances.

To Marco Tempest, Juan Mayoral and Norbert Ferré, because they are the guys I look up to in terms of magic and creativity.

To the greatest Magician, who is up there taking care of all of us.

To all those who contributed something, and who unfortunately time made me forget about you.

And finally, to You, for buying this book and for caring about my work. I sincerely hope you will enjoy it for many years.

From my heart, thanks a million!

Printed in Great Britain
by Amazon